CAREFUL-ISH

A Ridiculous Romp Through COVID-Living As Seen Through The Eyes Of Ridiculous People

Honey Parker

Published by Slow Burn

COPYRIGHT

To the one and only Ina Cohn—because I said so.

THE PROLOGUE HITS THE FAN

OUT IN PUBLIC

"No way out. No way out. None."

Benji has his head in his hands. He's sitting at a round-top bar table with four of his twenty-something friends. The bar is not quite a dive. More dive-*ish*. Just dive-like enough to make a white-collar worker feel gritty. Even when he's sitting, you can tell that this white guy is oddly tall. He also looks a bit like Kylo Ren, but without the cool. His focus on fretting is intense.

"No damn way out. I see no way out." Is it a chant? A mantra? A rant? A rantra?

Sitting next to him is Shad, a good-looking black guy, and the best dressed of this fivesome in a dark green business suit. "It's not that bad, man. Not end-of-world bad."

Benji just continues, "There's. No. Way. Out."

"Seriously, dude. We all lost money. I lost money."

Even if Benji wanted to stop, he knows he can't. This is part of him. His shrink calls it a spiral. It'll keep going until it doesn't. Now he whispers, "Nooo waaay ow-T!"

Kimi, Asian, with an artsy/industrial vibe, is as abrupt as she is short. She's wearing her own stress on her sleeve. She leans to Benji. "Look, Sunshine. At least you still have a job. I've got a hundred pounds of rotting pansies in a ten-by-ten apartment that, just by the way, I can no longer afford. No work. No prospects. And my place smells like Yankee Stadium after a hard rain and a long pee."

The other four all look at Kimi, confused. She concedes, "It made more sense before I said it out loud."

Jackson is handsome and buff with a smoky, Middle Eastern look. He raises his glass. "My friends, it will all be fine. Winter is past. We have beer. And my hair is luscious again, thanks to you, Joy."

Joy is an electric eclectic in flowing colors with bleached white hair in big, hot-roller curls. Heavy-*ish*, she has the air of a woman confident that her sexual appetite equals her sex appeal. Breaking into Jackson's toast, she says, "You forgot the, 'The.'"

His beer still in the air, Jackson raises an eyebrow. "Excuse me?"

"I'm now identifying as The Joy. Not just *some* Joy. *The* Joy."

Kimi snarks. "You were serious about that shit?"

"I'm always serious."

With a playful smirk, Jackson points at The Joy. "No, you're not."

"Well, yeah. Unless I'm not."

Shad is just confused. "That means nothing."

In rushes Steph, moving as fast as her bronze pencil skirt will allow. Her white blouse billows in the moderate breeze she creates. An attractive brunette, she carries a briefcase that costs as much as a mortgage payment, and has files under her arm. She grabs Jackson's beer, thrusts it to her lips, sucks it down and sputters. She turns to him. "Light beer? Seriously?"

Shad cracks, "He's watching your waistline."

Benji mumbles, "Just no way out."

Steph looks with curiosity at Benji. Shad says, "He's in a spiral."

"Again?"

Shad turns to Benji, "Dude, we *all* lost money."

Steph says, "Not me."

Shad turns. "What?"

"I didn't lose money...Well, not *lose* lose. We knew it was coming. My advisor kept enough parked on the side to take advantage of the buy-back."

With a sudden look of steely knives, Shad looks askance, drinks his beer, and stares at Steph.

Kimi claps her hands in front of Benji's face. "Sunshine! Join us!"

Steph is still fixated on her own narrative. "Things at the network are crazy pants. Cray-Z-Pants. Crazy! My group's taking shifts in the office now. Seriously, news in shifts? How does that work? The clock strikes whenever and I just hand off my shit to whoever? Where's the continuity? And is *that* even safe enough? Then again, Bill's whole team is all on, all the time. Is that a huge mistake? Serious crazy. Granted, distancing from Janis is a bonus, but..." Steph turns to The Joy and whips out a slice of counterfeit charm. "Joy! Can you give me a quick trim before everything shuts down?"

"The."

"Hmm?"

"It's, *The* Joy. With a 'The.'"

"You meant that?"

Kimi says, "Oh, she meant it." She swigs her beer.

Shad takes his turn at self-involved. "Janis sounds like a peach compared to Max. Try working for a guy who, at any second, could spontaneously combust."

Jackson adds, "Well, you have to love a man who legally changes his name from Maximillian to Maxabillion. Brilliant."

"Do I?"

"You do." Finish line in sight, Steph cuts off Shad. "*The* Joy, what do you say? Things are gonna get very serious very soon. My hair is beyond serious length."

Shad looks concerned. Steph is in news. She knows things before normal people. "How serious?"

"About a half inch."

"No, gorgeous. Not your hair."

"Oh. Oh! That. *Serious*, serious. We could be going the way of Italy any second."

SNEEZE! Someone at the next table. It's like a needle-scratch on a record. Everyone in the joint stops and swivels to face the germ-spreader. Mr. Sneezer, face in his elbow, looks up sheepishly. He glances around at everyone staring daggers in his direction. He wipes his nose with a cocktail napkin, then pockets it. With care and suspicion, everyone slowly resumes their drinking lives.

Doing his best Mussolini, Benji exclaims, "Nessuna via d'uscita!"

Shaking her head, Kimi says, "Sunshine says what?"

Benji answers, "Nessuna via d'uscita. It's Italian for..."

Jackson cuts in, "No way out."

Benji turns. He and Jackson give each other the secret-society nod and smile.

Shad's thrown by all of this. He knows Benji and Jackson have an otherworld he's not a part of. In a bad Italian accent that smacks of cultural appropriation, he says, "And you know that for to why?"

Benji shrugs. "Perchè no?"

Jackson toasts Benji. "Exactly!"

The Joy is delighted. "This is fun!"

Still in her own world of hair, Steph asks, "Seriously. *The* Joy. Can you fit me in?"

"Perchè no?" The Joy is now excited by contributing to the game. "Oh, I love this!"

Kimi turns her beer bottle upside down and looks around the table. "Another round?"

Shad asks, "You buying?"

"You kidding? I bought the last one with my electric-bill payment."

With genuine concern, The Joy leans to Kimi. "Listen, lady, if you're in a bind, you can always stay with me."

Benji almost does a spit take. "That's funny."

Both women are about to give Benji shit, but the big tip bell rings, loud and fast. The bartender steps out from behind the dinged-up wood bar. She's small, and no question a force to be feared. You could lose a digit.

Most of the room stops talking and turns to look. The bartender, loud but without yelling, announces, "Hey! Hey! Shut up. This just in. We're being shut down. All restaurants and bars are closed 'til further notice. You don't have to go home. But you can't stay here. Oh, wait. Yeah, you have to go home. New York City is under quarantine. Go home! Don't forget to tip your wait staff."

Surprised chatter washes over the bar. Shad's the first of the gang to become incredulous. "No. Wait. What?"

Steph panics. "Oh, my God. My hair!"

In his native desert tongue, Benji swears with color and venom. Then, with drama, "And now, *I'm* out of work. Thank you all for snapping me from my spiral for this tasty shot of reality."

The bar crowd starts to dissipate. Jackson scoops up several beers from their table, then a few more from a table that was just vacated. "Bonus beers!"

Slow and reluctant, the group gets up. They don't want to leave. Shad is still trying to make sense of it all. "I can't believe this. We're quarantining! No weekly beer meet-ups?"

The Joy is reflective. "This is so sad." A thoughtful pause, then, "Hey, wait. We don't have to isolate from each other. We can...no, we can do our beer meet-ups on a video call...Next week. Our regular meet-up time. Yes. We have to." Somber, the others mumble agreement. But The Joy is definitive. "It's a date, then! Next week, 5 p.m.! And Kimi, really, if you need a place to stay, The Joy has the room."

Kimi turns to her, "So now we're moving on from unnecessary articles to the third person? Look, totally appreciated. Really. But The Kimi will be just fine. Me and my pee-stink pansies will be just fine."

LOCKDOWN/DAY ONE

THE JOY'S APARTMENT

The door to The Joy's apartment flings open so hard, it slams into the wall. Oops. Kimi is standing there, loaded down with a suitcase, two backpacks and an arm full of dying flowers. "Sorry."

The Joy is standing in the kitchen area. She looks up from her tea mug. Her Chelsea brownstone apartment is eclectic, with lots of color and odd knick-knacks. Really odd. Like the nude mannequin missing its torso. Just limbs and a head, all suspended in their proper place. The "open space" is a clutter fest. Yet, in its odd way, everything seems to have a place.

In her self-protective way, Kimi announces, "This is just for a little bit."

The Joy says "Lady, you can stay as long as you need to...or a month."

Kimi scans the apartment, thrown by the visual overwhelm. And perhaps the lack of cleanliness. Kimi carefully picks up a strange object and studies it. It's a white, baby doll body with a black baby doll head.

The Joy rushes over. "That can't be moved...or touched."

Kimi drops the doll. "Sorry. Didn't know."

The Joy carefully picks up the doll and whispers in its ear, "Don't worry, Pinchy. You're fine." She puts the doll back in her place and looks at Kimi. "It's all part of my juju."

"Your what-what?"

"My juju. Everything manages a particular energy in the place it's in. You move a piece, you move the energy."

"So I shouldn't touch anything."

The Joy snaps right back to her regular level of happy. "That works for me."

Something in a corner falls over and breaks. Kimi's head snaps around. "What the hell was that? Is this place haunted? I can't move into a haunted place."

"Wouldn't that be cool? No, that was The Fred, my cat."

"Well, the cat just monkeyed with your juju."

"It's OK. We needed an energy shift."

"So when the cat moves something, energy shift. Got it. So much to learn…Where should I put my stuff?"

The Joy heads to a corner of the apartment. "I laid out this whole corner for you." She waves Kimi over. "Come here. Over here."

After a long pause, Kimi slowly makes her way through the room, careful not to touch anything. The Joy beams with excitement. Kimi's new corner has a La-Z-Boy, a frilly lamp, a battered night stand and a mini fridge with a scarf over it. The Joy's eyes widen. "How about this?"

Kimi takes it in and slowly nods. "A girl could get spoiled."

The Joy sweeps her arm over the space as she gives Kimi the tour without needing to take a step. "Your bed…your lighting…clothing storage…kitchen…and there's more!"

"Have I earned more?"

The Joy reaches up and pulls a shower curtain across the corner. It's on a curved shower-curtain rod like the kind found in every hotel bathroom. She's closed Kimi behind the curtain and calls out, "Privacy!"

Behind the curtain, Kimi stands and wonders how her life has come to this. Will it be possible for her immigrant parents, whose sole purpose in life is to push their children into professional careers, to ever stop giving her passive aggressive shit? Or plain old, flat out, confrontational shit? Emotionlessly she says to herself, "I should have been a dentist."

STEPH'S APARTMENT

It's evening and Steph is alone in her small but sharply appointed, Upper East Side apartment. It's very clean with a few key, personal touches. There are a few pictures from favorite trips and several silver serving pieces that belonged to her grandmother. The art on the walls represent the types of pieces she's likely to own as originals, some day. The blue light from her computer, along with the city light flowing in from the window wall illuminate the space.

Steph sits back from her computer, which is on her dining room table. It's clear that not much eating happens on this table. After a long, exhausted stare at the screen, she gets up and walks to the fridge. She opens the door and just stares inside. Zero inspiration.

JACKSON'S APARTMENT

Jackson, with his head in his refrigerator, is perusing the "Bonus beer." Which one? Which one? He spots a winner and grabs it. Happiness.

THE JOY'S APARTMENT

The Joy is staring into her fridge looking for inspiration. A small crash happens in a far corner.

Kimi calls from behind the curtain, "What was that?"

The Joy smiles to herself. *Oh, that The Fred.*

KIMI'S CORNER

Kimi is nestled in the La-Z-Boy in her private corner with the curtain closed. She surveys her new home. All of her few things are in their place, and her flowers have been arranged in several coffee cans which now sit on top of the fridge, nightstand and a suitcase. Kimi leans over from her adjustable seating and contorts herself so she can peek into the fridge. Empty. What did she expect?

In her state of "what the hell has happened to my life," she stays hanging upside down for some time and feels the blood rush to her head. Feels pretty okay.

SHAD & BENJI'S APARTMENT

Shad and Benji's apartment is what can be called, in New York City, a two-bedroom. Actually, it's a one bedroom with a lofted space over the kitchen that can, and always is, turned into a second bedroom. Benji is in the kitchen holding the fridge door open and staring inside. It's a hodge-podge of plastic food containers and beer. Shad comes up, reaches past Benji and grabs himself a beer. Benji turns his head slowly and stares at Shad.

Shad shrugs. "What?" He keeps moving and drops onto the sofa, which is flanked by a large club chair and sits in front of a coffee table and flat screen. Douglas, a smallish boxer-mix jumps onto the sofa next to him to get petted. Shad hits on the TV. News. No. He switches to Bloomberg. No. Sports reruns. Safe.

Benji glares at him the entire time and finally says, "Nothing."

Shad has to think for a moment about what was said that prompted that answer. Oh, yeah. "Oh, it's something."

Benji turns back to the fridge. His lack of words is very loud.

Shad snaps. "You blame me."

Benji pulls a beer for himself then grabs food and starts prepping to cook. Without looking at Shad, he says overly innocent, "What would I blame you for?"

"Just say it."

"Say what?"

"Oh, I don't know...That you're mad at me that you're down a four-handle. Excuse me. 40K. That you think I'm a crappy money manager. That you should have pulled more out sooner. That I should be fired. That my life is a sham and the only purpose I serve is to take the hard-fought earnings of people like you and turn them into an empty pit of despair."

"Okay. That."

"I can't believe you said that, bro."

"You said that."

"But you agreed."

Benji gives a self-satisfied shrug. "Mmm."

An uncomfortable silence ensues as Benji starts cooking. He clearly knows what he's doing. Lots of fast chopping, spices being added and pan flipping. For some people, this is the magic that only chefs can pull off. For Benji, it's automatic. He's a savant. He tastes, adjusts, and tastes again. Good.

Shad can't take the silence any more. He blurts out, "Look, life is chance. Didn't you

take a chance leaving mathematics for cooking? I supported you. I was nothing but supportive. This is a bump. We knew it was coming. This could be so much worse."

Benji doesn't stop what he's doing. He just says flatly, "Really? How?"

"A...you could have freaked and totally pulled out. Which would be much worse. B...you could be Jackson."

"I could be a handsome, buff actor who gets all the girls."

Shad gets up and walks to the kitchen. "You could be a handsome, buff actor...who has never made a dime acting, lives alone and has zero, zero chance of paying his bills. My money says Jackson moves in with Kimi and The Joy within a week."

"Well, who could argue with your money?" Benji smells what's in the pan, approves, and slides it into the dog bowl. "Douglas." Douglas comes over and attacks the food.

JACKSON'S APARTMENT

Jackson is now lying on a quilted leather sofa in a dark room watching a sci-fi super-fan channel on YouTube on his phone. He turns an empty beer bottle upside-down. Bummer. He reaches down to the floor and gropes without looking. Finally, Jackson's fingers locate another beer bottle. Success.

STEPH'S APARTMENT

Steph is in her living room, standing at her window looking out over the night sky, cocktail in hand. The news is on low in the background. Nothing good. She's alone and conflicted. She knows that this pandemic could be gold for her career. She wishes for something, then feels guilty for her wish. She takes it back. But not really.

THE JOY'S APARTMENT

The Joy is at her kitchen counter. She drains the last of her deep-red cocktail. It's rimmed with all manner of flair. Plastic monkeys, giraffes, a lizard... She takes the cherry from the glass and lays it next to the other cherries that came before. What next?

She has an idea. The Joy mixes up another cocktail. This one is more aqua-marine in color. As she moves the flair from the last cocktail to the new one, she whispers a message to each plastic animal.

KIMI'S CORNER

Kimi is passed out in her La-Z-Boy with an empty beer bottle and a stuffed monkey on her chest. In its current position, it looks like the monkey drank the beer.

She dreams of having a giant tulip as her boss. Her tulip boss is not happy. As it accuses her of not being nice enough to customers, its petals begin drying up and falling off. Finally, she's being reprimanded by a giant stem.

STEPH'S APARTMENT/BEDROOM

The light from Steph's bathroom seeps into her bedroom. Her cell rings. She comes out of the bathroom in her pajamas. They're comfy but cute, and probably not cheap. She looks around the room and finds her cell in the bed covers. She stares at the caller I.D. for a moment and reluctantly answers it. "Janis? It's late. What's up?"

Through the phone Janis replies, "Click video."

"What?"

"Click video. I want to video chat."

Steph looks around the room as if to see if anyone's watching. She straightens up her pajamas, flips and adjusts her hair, then presses video. "Okay."

Janis's face appears on Steph's screen. She's in her fifties and looks like she just got out of bed. She also looks like she could take you down. She can. Janis has been around the block, more than a few times, fighting the whole way. "Big news. You're interviewing Justin Mac tomorrow. He has coronavirus!"

Steph is baffled. "Wait, what? Me? How? Why isn't Jim taking this? Justin's huge."

"Jim's too important to get coronavirus."

"Wow. I'm flattered."

Janis, sounding like a movie from the forties says, "This could be a big win for you."

"A big win that could kill me."

"In news there are always downsides...Oh, bring a mask with you...Something cute." And just like that, Janis hangs up. The screen goes black.

Steph looks around the room again. Still no one there. Then a sudden, sobering thought. "My hair."

JACKSON'S APARTMENT

Jackson is shirtless and lit by the glow of his phone screen in an otherwise completely dark room. The phone is balanced on his crossed legs. He's watching a comedian on YouTube and laughing. This time, he's on a different sofa.

As he watches the video, he absently plays with a pen on his lower lip. He proceeds to get the pen stuck. "Ow!" No harm. No foul. He keeps watching.

SHAD & BENJI'S APARTMENT/LOFT

Benji is in his lofted bedroom asleep under a Spiderman bedspread. He dreams of hanging out with Scott Conant after having just won an episode of *Chopped*. When Benji wakes, he won't remember his success.

SHAD & BENJI'S APARTMENT/SHAD'S BEDROOM

Shad's lying awake under his 1200-count sheets with Douglas by his side. The room is small. His queen bed almost touches the desk. His treadmill peeks out from under the bed. He keeps having conversations in his head. Something Shad does a lot. The problem with that is, he never gives the other person in his self-scripted conversations anything nice to say to him. This time it's his father. An imposing but affable man in a sweater. In Shad's mind, he's sitting in his father's study.

His dad says, "You know son, you had the speed and the brains to play running back. I always said that, didn't I? And you would have learned to take a hit. That's important in life. But you wanted finance. And I didn't stop you. I'd never stand in my son's way. Any of you. But look at you now. You took a hit. A big one. Maybe finance isn't your game. Sometimes you want the game but that game doesn't want you. Think about that...And son, that green suit just looks stupid on you. Think about that."

Shad thinks about it all.

BRAVE NEW DAY

THE JOY'S APARTMENT

It's morning. Kimi emerges from her corner dressed for the day, which for her is nothing fancy, but neat and intentional. She has her own flair and it works in an industrial florist kind of way. She looks around the apartment thinking how the entire space seems to morph based on the changing light of the day.

She feels a vibration in her hand and realizes that she'd been talking on her cell. Shit. "One more time?"

Kimi's long-time, girlfriend Carmen says, "Are you even listening to me?

"Yes. What? I'm right here."

"Well?"

"Well...I'm at The J's now."

"She meant that shit?"

"Oh, she meant it."

"Well, is she gonna charge you?

"I don't know."

"Well, how much could you pay?"

"I don't know."

"Well..."

Kimi cuts her off, "I don't know that either."

The Joy comes out of her bedroom wearing a thin, flowing robe which floats behind her as she to heads to the kitchen. She has an odd nobility.

Kimi says quietly into her cell, "Listen, The J is on the move. I gotta go."

Carmen attempts to add, "Well, tell her I say..."

"Gotta go."

Kim pockets her cell and approaches The Joy in the kitchen area. But not too close. "Morning. Hey, uh, thanks again for letting me crash."

The Joy looks troubled. "You broke something?"

"No, I meant..."

"Kimi, I'm kidding with you. Chillax."

On edge, Kimi says, "Oh, yeah. Right. Sure."

"I can be funny. I don't know why you guys think I'm not funny." As The Joy talks, she fills a bowl with a bizarre selection of food items, then pours milk over it all. Kimi is fascinated. The Joy sees Kimi staring. "My bad. You want some of this?"

"Can you name it?"

The Joy thinks for a moment. "I can not."

"If I cannot name it, I cannot eat it."

The Joy heads to the sofa and sits with her feet up on the mod, oval-shaped coffee table and her breakfast treat on her lap. "So what are you going to do with your new-found downtime?"

"Slowly lose my mind."

"That sounds fun."

Kimi finds a banana in a bowl on the counter, and after careful inspection deems it safe-*ish*. She responds, "Doesn't it? No. I don't know. Not a lot of call for flower arranging at the moment. Perhaps when funerals become all the rage again."

"That's morbid...No offense, but you never struck me as the floral type."

"Really? What type did I strike you as?"

"You're more of the throat punch type. And, by the way, that's not an Asian thing. It's more of a, you-scare-people thing."

Kimi hops up on a kitchen bar stool and keeps things sarcastic. "Well, when I didn't get into the WWE, I fell back on flowers. Seemed the obvious choice. Now, who knows. Perhaps gum surgery. Or maybe I'll just go online and see what's out there for an underachieving, first-gen, scary person."

.   Trying to make Kimi feel better, The Joy offers, "Hey, at least you're not Jackson. I have no idea how he..." she makes air quotes, "covers his end."

"I could never figure out how he..." Kimi copies The Joy's quotes, "covers his end. Has he ever had one acting job? Or one audition?"

"I assumed he lives off the kindness of strangers. Nudge, nudge. Wink, wink."

"There won't be a lot of stranger action during the coronavirus lockdown."

Kimi thinks about how much sexual activity she can look forward to in the near future. Carmen is in Miami, so things don't look promising.

JACKSON'S APARTMENT

Jackson is on his feet in front of a computer. He's in shorts and a tight-fitting tank top dancing to an online workout class. Everyone in the class is female. Jackson has all the energy and abandon of the "Carlton Dance" from *The Fresh Prince of Bel Air*. It's all so, very 80s.

STEPH'S APARTMENT

Stephanie busts through the front door of her apartment and drops her stuff right there. Without breaking stride, she walks through the living room and heads straight to the bedroom. As she walks through the bedroom, she removes her clothes—everything but her mask. But where to put her togs? It's like they're suddenly too dirty to leave anywhere. After spinning several times, she finally settles on a corner of the floor and b-lines into the bathroom.

A moment later she's standing in the shower, eyes closed, holding onto the wall. "Fuck." Wet mask.

SHAD & BENJI'S APARTMENT/BATHROOM

Shad is on the commode with a section of the Wall Street Journal. He's wearing a nice button down shirt and has jog pants around his ankles. He absently reaches over to the toilet paper roll. Damn it! The end of the role. From his seat, he reaches open the vanity under the sink. Nothing. Damn it!

Shad hears scratches at the door. He watches incredulously as Douglas pushes his way into the bathroom, heads directly for a litter box that's set in the corner and steps in. He does his business, makes a few gestures at covering it up with his back legs and meanders out without ever looking up at Shad. That's just great.

From his seat, Shad looks around. Nothing resembling toilet paper. Finally, he rips a newspaper page, crinkles it up and checks its readiness. Not yet. More crinkling. He checks again. Not yet. More crinkling. He checks again, Just right. Finally satisfied, he looks around, as if someone might be watching him in the bathroom, then wipes.

KIMI'S CORNER

Kimi is in the La-Z-Boy with her computer on her lap. She's checking out the rising number of virus cases. New York is exploding. What the what? Her anxiety is like a ball of food that she can't swallow. Two sirens go past the building. Should she get up? Buy cleaning supplies? Cough medicine? A flack-jacket? She checks her forehead to see if she has a fever.

Without thinking, she farts then suddenly realizes that she's potentially not alone. She's not used to her new living situation. This sucks. She looks around, then thinks to herself, "I think I got away with that...Bullet dodged." She has a small smile at the minor victory, then goes back to surfing the bad news.

STEPH'S APARTMENT/BEDROOM

Steph wanders into her bedroom from the bathroom. She's damp and wrapped in a towel. Confused she stands in front of her bureau and looks at herself in the mirror for a long moment. She thinks to herself, "Was that worth it? Is this my springboard to a big career?" She looks at her hands which are pressed on the top of her bureau so hard that her fingertips are white. She heads back to the bathroom.

From her bedroom, the sound of the shower turning back on can be heard. No one is there to hear it.

SHAD & BENJI'S APARTMENT

Benji is on the sofa playing jazz guitar to an online lesson. He's not so good. Shad's dog, Douglas, jumps onto the sofa with him. Benji gives up on the guitar and uses the remote to turn on the TV. An earnest news anchor shares nothing but bad news. Benji turns it off and stares into space. He absently picks his nose, looks around and flicks it across the room. He looks at Douglas and with a finger, motions, "Shh."

Shad comes into the room looking rather put out. Without really looking at him, Benji says, "You've been gone a while."

"Don't act like you didn't know where I was.

"Weren't you in the little broker's booth?"

"You know what I mean."

"What?"

"You stranded me. A real friend would have brought me a roll of TP."

"A, you didn't ask..."

"Don't act like you didn't know."

"B, we're out of TP as is the bodega. C..."

Exasperated with this new news, Shad cuts Benji off. "They're out? Damn it. You were supposed to stock up. Now we have to go the market."

Benji wasn't done. "C! There's still a C. A real friend would make good on the money he made his real friend lose on his advice."

Shad's fed up. He explodes. "There is no C. C is bullshit. C has left the building. This is the death of C. C can fuck itself. That's not how it works. No one, *no one* came out of the crash untouched. I did my best. And this thing is far from over. Did others do better..?

Benji says, "Yes."

"A...you don't know that. B...we'll come back. We will. I told you that. What do I always say? What are the three things you can always count on? Death, taxes and regression to the mean."

"And what is the mean? Which mean? Is it the mean from ten years ago? Is it the mean from yesterday? Those are two totally different means. The conditions under which regression toward the mean occurs depend on the way the term is mathematically defined. So, define. Define your conditions for me."

Shad can't believe he's having to deal with this in his own home. It's like having a client with 24-hour access. "Ah! Stop. The mean is stability. Things are unstable in the short term but quite stable in the long term. The market will regress, and the restaurant business will regress. You think New Yorker's are going to give up restaurants? No. Never happen. We just have to wait this out. In a few months, we'll all be back out eating and drinking like normal people. And you'll have a job. You're a hell of a cook. It'll work out."

Benji asks Douglas, "Do you see this working out, Douglas?" The dog barks. "Douglas says, he doesn't see it."

JACKSON'S APARTMENT

Jackson is staring at himself in a wall mirror as he strategically places strips of clear tape on his face. With one strip, he raises an eyebrow. With another strip, he pulls his nose to the left. With the next strip he lifts his lip, giving himself a sneer that is part Elvis, part thug. Jackson admires his work. Not bad. His smile rips a piece of tape out of place. No problem. He has plenty more.

THE JOY'S APARTMENT

The Joy is on the sofa, examining her own hair and snipping little pieces off. There's a buzz at the door. With scissors still at the ready, she goes to the door and hits the intercom. "What?"

Over the bad intercom, a male voice says, "PackageGuys."

The Joy calls back, "You don't sound like Mike. Is this Mike?"

"No. I'm Vlad."

Hmm. Intriguing. "Really? Where's Mike?"

"Mike moved. I have this route now."

"Tell me more."

"I have a package here for a...It says for, The Joy?"

Cautiously, The Joy caves, "Okay...Vlad. I'll give you a chance. But only because I need to know what a Vlad looks like."

She hits the button that unlocks the door to the building. Being in a ground-floor apartment, it just takes a moment before there's a knock at the door.

As if she has no former knowledge of who's visiting, The Joy answers, "Who is it?"

"Vlad, from PackageGuys."

The Joy slowly opens her front door like she's unwrapping a present. Vlad, the PackageGuys man, is wearing a mask and holding a small package and an electronic clipboard. No need to ask Vlad if he works out. Vlad's biceps and pecks are stretching his uniform to the limit. The Joy eyes him up and down, clearly happy with what she sees. They exchange sexy looks. The Joy looks over at Kimi's corner. Quiet. This could work out.

KIMI'S CORNER

Kimi has become one with her La-Z-Boy. With her feet up and computer on her lap, she's like something from a futuristic novel. She's reviewing her bank account. This is bad. In her head, she does the math on how long before she has absolutely nothing. She's down to weeks...maybe.

Kimi grabs her phone, stares at it, gets mad, then puts it down again. Shit. Shit. Shit.

While considering other options, she absently digs in her ear. She pulls something out. She examines the dry bit of wax, looks around and realizes there's no trash can in her corner. Finally, she places the wax on her night stand to dispose of later. This sucks so much.

STEPH'S APARTMENT

Steph is at her desk/dining table on her computer with her cell in her hand. She flips her hair, as she does before every call, even if it's just audio, hits the call button and places the cell in the phone cradle on the table.

After a lot of rings, an older female voice picks up. "Hello, New York."

Ever since Steph moved to New York from South Jersey, her mother has answered the phone that way. Steph's used to it, but finds it just a bit annoying. Her mother's accent isn't New York. It's part Philly, part New Jersey and all Jewish. Resigned to her mother's quirks, Steph responds, "Hey, Mom. How's it going?'

Ida starts the way she often does, "We're fine. Your father's making me crazy."

Steph asks, "...er?"

Ida's confused, "What?''

"Nothing. What's he doing?"

"He's just sitting there, like he always does. But when I ask him to get the phone, he picks up his book and tells me he's reading."

"Is the phone ringing a lot?'

"No. No one calls here. It's like we're dead."

Steph considers pointing out that if no one is calling, it can't be that big of a problem, but thinks better of it. Logic is rarely helpful with her parents. Moving on. "So Mom, are you ready to do this?

"I don't think I need to Zoom. Why can't we just talk?

"Don't you want to see me? Who knows how long quarantine's gonna last.

There's a long silence. Finally her mom acquiesces, "Fine. Just go slow. You know I'm not good with computers."

"OK, Mom. You're at your computer, right?"

"Of course, I am."

"So you got the Zoom invite in your email?"

"I have it right here. It's open."

Surprised, Steph says, "Great. Great. Click the link. It's in blue."

In her measured cadence Ida says, "I see something that says, w, e, r, t, 4, t, w..."

Steph cuts her off, "That's it, Mom. Just click it."

"OK, I did that."

"Now, do you see the click that says, join the conversation?"

Back to her cadence, Ida reads her from screen, "I see file. I see edit."

"No. Mom, not the top of the computer. Did a window come up after you clicked the email link?

"Yes."

"The join button is in that window."

"I see view. I see help..."

Steph's frustration is hard to keep at bay. "Mom. Stop."

"I thought you wanted to do the Zoom."

"I do. But you have to listen to me."

"I'm listening. Who's not listening? I've heard everything you've said."

Steph's father's semi-annoyed voice comes over the speaker, but from further away. He speaks in the volume that people use when they don't hear well. "Ida, what are you doing?"

Ida responds to her husband, "I'm Zooming with your daughter."

Steph's father, Murray, or Mur as Ida calls him, questions her, "You're what?

"Zooming. It's like a phone call but with video. You want to see your daughter?

"I know what she looks like."

Ida's voice is addressed back to Steph. "Your father's not joining."

Steph does her best to not lose it. She's had years of practice.

JACKSON'S APARTMENT

Jackson, with tape on his face, making him look pig-like, is dressed in sheets draped to look reminiscent of a *Star Wars* character. He's standing in front of a computer screen and holding a lightsaber. The light from the screen is the only light in the room, adding to the sci-fi mood.

A voice from in the computer says, "Your size is your weakness." It's a kid. Jackson is doing *Star Wars* cos-play with a Middle Eastern teenager.

In character voice, Jackson responds, "...And your overconfidence is yours."

THE JOY'S APARTMENT

The Joy is at the front door with Vlad, the PackageGuys guy. He's tucking in his shirt. In her sexiest voice she whispers to him, "Well, you have a blessed day." She raises an eyebrow and smirks. He leers from over his mask. She can feel it. After a long look, he leaves and she closes the door slowly.

Kimi abruptly throws open her curtain, startling The Joy. "I smell cologne. Did you just have someone here?"

The Joy tries to appear casual. "Oh, that was just the new PackageGuys guy."

Kimi is incredulous. "Aren't we supposed to be maintaining social distance?

"That's why I'm having my packages delivered, silly. I'm not going out in public.

Kimi, making air quotes at key moments, responds, "Yeaaaaah. But you're not supposed to be "handling" someone else's "packages" either. "Nudge, nudge. Wink, wink."

"Oh, that. Well, that's what Purell is for, right? And I really think you're overdoing the air quotes thing. They lose their potency after like the third one."

"Wrong."

"No. They do."

Trying to measure how pissed she lets herself sound, Kimi says, "I don't give a shit about air quotes. Look, I appreciate you letting me stay here. I do. But what you just did wasn't safe."

"You know I'm on the pill."

"Oh, my God! Nooooo. It's not coronavirus safe." Kimi, moves from measured pissed to measured exasperated. "And if you bring something into this apartment, I could catch it, too. Look, it's your life. Live it. I'll find somewhere else to stay."

The Joy has to sit and think about this for a long moment. "Oh, my God. This is gonna suck."

"Right? See, now your life is as shitty as the rest of ours."

SHAD & BENJI'S APARTMENT

Benji's in the kitchen at the stove. He's got something going in a pan and skillfully flips it a few times. Shad looks over. "That smells good."

Benji pours the concoction into the dog bowl. He calls out, "Yo, Doug." The dog comes over and digs into his treat. Benji smirks at Shad.

Shad's done. "OK, this has lasted long enough."

Benji innocently, "What has?"

"What are you, five? Just stop it. I'm done. I give. Name your price."

Benji just stares at Shad. He's not ready to give. Shad wants terms. "Shy of a refund, which is impossible, what can I do to make things right with us?"

Benji thinks for a long moment then bends down to pet Douglas, who's still eating. Benji looks up at Shad. "Your dog."

"What?!"

Benji stands up straight. "I want your dog."

Shad looks at Benji trying to detect if he actually means it.

THE REST OF THE WEEK

STEPH'S APARTMENT

Steph is on a video cell call with Janis. She tries to strike her best mix of business-like and nonchalant. Even while dressed for work, Janis is unkempt looking. She also looks like she knows that she's too important to need to care about it. In her back-handed way, Janis says, "Saw the footage. You did ok-*ish.*"

Steph tries not to seem put out. "*Ish*?"

"Justin could have seemed sicker."

In her head, Steph says, "Seriously, bitch? I could have died. That guy was coughing up a storm, wouldn't wear a mask and was making out with his dog half the time. Where's my goddamn thank you?" Out loud she says, "Mmm."

"We're gonna need new wrap-arounds. We teed up for a really-sick guy. You're on that, right?"

"Yep."

"You'll make it happen ASAP, right?"

"Yep."

"Oh, and your hair isn't as serious as it could be."

JACKSON'S APARTMENT

Jackson is asleep in a big, cushy chair. His arm is draped over the side, a light-sabre is in his hand. There's a beer bottle on the floor next to him. Over his computer, there's the call of a Wookie. Jackson's hand reflexively raises the lightsaber and he jumps to his feet. He looks left, then right. He's alone. He thinks, "Take a breath, fella. You're safe."

SHAD & BENJI'S APARTMENT

Shad enters the living room and finds Benji is...dancing? Is that dancing? He's not in obvious pain, but this is off-putting. Benji takes up a lot of space and when he "dances," it makes you feel like you should look for cover. Shad realizes that Benji has his phone propped on the coffee table. The dog is on the sofa, watching. Shad asks, "What ya doin'?"

Benji keeps doing what he's doing and somewhat breathlessly answers, "TikTok. I think I'm getting it."

"Mmm, you're not...But it's good to have a goal."

"I couldn't watch the news anymore. The 6:00 p.m. panic report was making me crazy. You know what the death rate in the city is up to? Come on. Try this with me."

"Dude, TikTok's for teenage girls in the suburbs."

Still dancing, Benji says, "No. It's good."

"It's good? Where's your dignity, man?"

"Dignity's just an excuse to limit your joy. I was in marching band. I have no need for dignity. Come on. Get in on this...Come on. Fuck dignity in the face."

Shad thinks and then slowly walks to Benji's side of the coffee table. God, he hopes no one can see this, which, of course, they can't. "Does this mean we're okay now?"

"Maybe." Benji waits for the right moment in the TikTok dance. He prompts, "And...go." It's a spastic mess. Limbs everywhere. Both roommates are behind the beat. They bang their arms on each other. "Shit." It's over. Benji shakes his head and waits for the right moment to start again. He calls out, "And...go." And wow. That was no better.

They try the dance at least a dozen more times. Shad is starting to get better at it... Somewhat. On the next round, Benji accidentally kicks the coffee table, breaking one of the legs and the thing collapses. Shad stops short and is seemingly horrified. "Shit! That was my great grandmother's. It's the only thing I have from her."

Benji is now equally horrified, "Shit! Seriously?"

"No."

It often takes Benji a bit longer to realize he's being screwed with. After a few beats he finally catches on. "You're a dick."

"So we're good now?"

Benji completely acquiesces, "Yeah, we're good." And just that quickly, his focus is on his phone. "And...go."

THE JOY'S APARTMENT

Kimi walks through the apartment to the back window. She ponders what's before her. There are multiple pieces of juju on the sill. How is she going to maneuver her way out of the window and onto the fire escape without disturbing the energy? The Joy is on the sofa reading a book and makes no obvious signs of noticing Kimi, but Kimi can feel her eyes on her. She finally pulls over a chair, stands on it, and reaches over the juju to raise the window. Done. Next move. She ever so carefully steps between the treasures. It's like a minefield but with porcelain Japanese cats, a plastic alligator with Mardi Gras beads, and a miniature model hair salon in a bottle. Careful. Be careful...Success.

Kimi makes her way on to the fire escape, sits, and breathes in her first fresh air in days. Is that a light breeze? Damn, that's good. She looks around at the backs of other brownstones. She's not alone. People are minding their own business as they go about living their outdoor lives on tiny patches of metal. A few people are reading. A woman is feeding a baby. A guy attempts to play a clarinet. From the sound of it, he's revisiting the instrument for the first time in a long time. Most of the people just seem to be staring at nothing. The guy with the clarinet waves to her. Kimi raises a reluctant hand and nods. Not wanting to cause a friendship, she looks away and takes out her cell.

It's time to make her call. Shit, she doesn't want to make this call. There's at least two more minutes of staring at the phone before she pulls up Milli's number and hits the call button. Ring. Ring. Ring. Ring. Kimi's about to end the call when a voice answers abruptly.

"What!"

"Good to hear you, too." Kimi's not actually put out by this greeting. She and her sister Milli have been doing that to each other for years. Who started it? Probably Kimi. She kind of treasures the familiarity of their blunt ritual. She can't do it with her other sibling. They're too serious, or important. Not that Milli's not important. She just doesn't wear it like a badge.

Milli asks, "What's up? How are things at the House of Joy?"

"Mmm."

"That good?"

"It's fine. It's just... It's fine."

"Wow."

There's a long silence. Kimi is grasping for how she wants to proceed. Milli can't wait, "Just spill it."

Kimi chickens out. "How's work?"

"The hospital is crazy. No one knows how we're going to get ahead of this thing. We're getting zero guidance in regard to procedure and even less support. Thank you, administration. Oh, and people are yelling at us for enforcing protocols designed to save their lives. I have never seen anything like this. How do you put this in a class at medical school? I really don't see any end to this in the near future...Oh, and Shey's fine, the kids are fine, the dog is fine. What's wrong?"

Kimi sucks in her lips and says, "No big deal. I just have a bit of cash flow..."

"How much do you need?"

"Jesus! At least let me finish my groveling before you cut me off. I want to, on some level, feel like I earned it. Like it's not just that fucking easy for you to throw money around. Jesus, Milli. I hate when you do that."

"I apologize for not making you grovel."

"I forgive you."

"How much do you need?"

Dejected Kimi says, "I don't fucking know."

"God, Kimi. Your language. Did you swallow a sailor?"

"And I'm still hungry. Oh, was that racist? But really, I have this idea. I'm not just sitting on my ass. Well, I am sitting on my ass, a lot. But I've been thinking about how to be proactive about this thing."

"Spare me the gory details. I'll Venmo you tonight. It's not a problem."

"Hey, one more thing."

"Can I say, sure, or do you want to work for it?"

"Don't tell mom and pop about this. I can't handle the you-could-still-be-a-doctor speech right now."

"Not a word. Love you."

"Yeah." Kimi hangs up and becomes yet another person on a patch of metal, staring off at nothing.

JACKSON'S APARTMENT/HALLWAY

Jackson is bracing himself up off the ground. He's most of the way up the walls of a narrow hallway. He tries to look over at his watch and time this. Shit. How is he going to see his watch without letting go of the wall? Maybe if he does it quickly he can re-grab the wall in time? No. That won't work. Maybe he can hold himself up with just his feet? That could do it. He braces his feet extra hard against the wall and slowly pulls his hand from its touch point. Hey, this is working. He looks at his watch several times, clearly proud of himself. Then his leg grip gives just a bit and he slowly slides down the wall until he's just standing on the hall floor. Skid marks from his shoes are down both sides of the hall.

STEPH'S APARTMENT

Steph enters her front door. In addition to a nice long coat over her professional wear, she's wearing a mask and gloves. She's loaded down with her computer case and two large bags. The reusable kind that you get to carry a lot of groceries and not have strangers give you a hard time about using plastic. She's in get-it-done mode. Steph puts her computer bag on the dining table, drops the other large bags and removes her coat. As she's setting up her computer, her cell rings. She looks at the caller I.D. and considers whether she's going to answer. Finally, "Hey, Mom."

"Your father's making me crazy."

"What now?"

"He'll walk into a room and just start talking. Doesn't check to see if maybe I'm on the phone or watching a show."

"Mmm..."

"He just starts talking."

"Well..."

"It's his America."

   "Just..."

"Never thinks that maybe I'm in the middle of..."

Tired of this game, Steph interrupts, "Mom, listen, I have to rewrite something and it has to go out tonight."

Put out, Ida changes her tone. "I'm sorry I'm wasting your time again."

"No. Mom, you're not wasting my time. I'm not saying..."

Clearly hurt, and working the buttons she installed long ago, Ida says, "No, no. If you don't have time for your mother..."

Steph decides to break the no-win pattern of this conversation and takes a different tact—one she's used plenty of times in the past. "You're right. I don't have a spare moment for you. I only call when I need to kill time. I probably don't even really love you. I'm too busy to love the woman who gave me so much."

"I suppose you think you're funny."

"I know I'm funny."

"You get that from your father. He was always quick. And so handsome. You look like him, you know."

Steph's mood changes as her mother's mood changes. This dynamic has been going on all her life. "So I've heard."

"Oh, did you get the paper?"

Steph walks to the two large bags that she carried in and pulls a roll of toilet paper out. "I got it. I'll overnight it to you tomorrow."

"I don't want you to get in trouble."

"I won't...if I don't get caught. I'll overnight it to you."

"Not overnight. That's too much money. Just send it regular. We can hold on a few days...Probably."

"It's not too much money."

"This is so exciting. Ill-gotten toilet paper. I feel just like Thelma and Louise."

"I'm not going over a cliff with you, Mom."

SHAD & BENJI'S APARTMENT/BEDROOM

Shad's at his computer. He's dressed for work from the waist up. Below that, he's in boxer briefs. He's on a videoconference call with the team from his office. Everyone on the team looks to be in small, gray rooms. Kind of like closets. Behind them are flat, poorly-lit walls. A shelf here or there. Everyone except for his team leader, Max. Behind Max is a patio umbrella and a beautiful swimming pool surrounded by a manicured hedge. Max is on a rampage.

Max is mid-rage. "This is such fucking bullshit! Just because I was the first one smart enough to work remote, they think they can shove me into smaller offices? Fuck them. I don't care if I never set foot in the fucking building again. They're not taking my office. You know how much money I've made for them? Fuck them. This is such fucking bullshit!"

Shad, along with everyone else on the team quietly waits for this to pass. Avoiding eye contact feels like the right move.

Max shifts. "I so want good news. Someone. Give me something good. Make me proud. Sandra, who did you call today?"

Sandra, a serious looking gal with her hair pulled back, perhaps a bit too tightly, looks down.

"Give me a name. Who did you call? Just spit it out."

Trying to muster up any courage, but finding none, Sandra clears her throat and reports, "It's just, everyone is in such a weird mood right now, and I hoped that..."

Max goes red. "You hoped!? How many times have I said, hope is not a strategy? Anyone?" No one answers. Was that rhetorical? Max goes on. "This is totally unacceptable, people. I don't need any of you. My numbers alone are brilliant. Shiny silver brilliant. I don't have to have you four sucking off my profits. You clowns get a salary. Do I take a salary? Anyone? I don't! And I'm not going to carry your asses. You make your fucking plan and you work your fucking plan. It's that simple. This shit is coming back around like a slingshot. It's already started."

Benji leans in to Shad's room, oblivious to the brow-beating that's going on. He has a plate in his hand and says to Shad, "Five-cheese mac with crispy shrimp?"

Max is still ranting. "What do I always say? Death, taxes and regression to the mean! Say it. Death, taxes and regression to the mean."

Benji whispers to Shad, "Hey, he stole your line. That's your line."

Max is suddenly aware of Benji's presence and blurts, "Who is that guy? This is a private meeting. Who are you?"

Shad jumps in, "Uh, that's just my chef." He turns to Benji and as casually as possible says, "That will be all." Shad then tilts his head emphatically to Benji, motioning for him to leave."

Benji isn't thrilled, but takes the cue. On his way out he adds, "What a douche."

"What did he say?"

THE JOY'S APARTMENT

The Joy's on the sofa and completely sucked into a TV game show. Shouting at the screen she yells, "Taffeta! It's taffeta!" After a moment of silence, the show host says, "I'm sorry. The answer was taffeta." The Joy throws her hands up in the air. "I gave you the answer. You people never listen to me."

There's a buzz at the door and The Joy jumps to her feet. As she heads to the door she looks over to reassure herself that Kimi's curtain is closed. It is. She pushes the intercom and quietly answers, "Yes?"

Over the speaker a voice crackles, "It's Hope."

The Joy shushes her. In a whisper, "I'm buzzing you in. Now shush, you."

The Joy stays by the door. She cracks it open and watches Hope enter the hallway. When Hope gets to the apartment, The Joy pulls her in by the arm.

Hope is a fit, 40-something woman, dressed in workout togs. The kind everyone wears as regular clothes. She says, "Thanks for making room for me."

The Joy looks around again. "Shh. I don't want my boarder to hear us."

Hope lowers her voice, "Oh, I get it. Sure. Keeping it on the down low. Well, my hair thanks you."

"Your hair is welcome."

Hope, still in a whisper, "It wasn't easy navigating the line outside your building."

"That's for the market madness." She motions to her bedroom and becomes spa-like in her manner. "Come on into my salon. Would you like cucumber water?"

They disappear into The Joy's bedroom. Kimi pokes her head out from behind her curtain. The look on her face says she's not happy.

SHAD & BENJI'S APARTMENT

Benji is in the living room, attempting his TikTok dance again. This time, however, he's holding a plate of five-cheese mac with crunchy shrimp. The plate of food does not make him any better at the dance. As he pops a shrimp in his mouth, he sees his new dog eyeing the food. Benji pulls the rest of the shrimp off the dish and puts the plate on the floor.

Shad comes out of his bedroom announcing, "Well that sucked. Hey, I'll try that mac and cheese now." Benji shrugs and Shad sees the dog eating the food. He throws his hands up. Could this day get worse?

REUNION

KIMI'S CORNER

Kimi is in her La-Z-Boy with a colorful drink by her side. There's not much alcohol in the drink. It's more mixer than hooch, but the idea of having an adult beverage makes her feel better. She's drinking and texting with Carmen. "The J is going to be patient zero. I swear."

Carmen responds, "You okay?"

"I don't know...yes."

"Hang in there, baby girl."

"No, you. [Smile emoji]"

"Emojis are so last millennium.

"[Poop emoji]"

The Joy, brimming with perk, flings aside the shower curtain with cocktails in hand. "Knock, knock."

Kimi holds up her phone. "I'm texting here."

The Joy doesn't seem to notice her boarder's mood. "It's time."

"For...?"

"Cocktails with the gang!"

"Right. Forgot. One sec." She looks back at her phone and is about to text, but realizes that The Joy hasn't left. She just stands there beaming. Kimi gets incredulous. "Oh, my God. Did you not hear the *one sec*? I'll be there in one sec."

"OK. See you soon. Now, don't get lost." She laughs at her own joke.

Kimi stares at her until she's gone. She goes back to texting. "Must cocktail with The J. More later. [Nine random emojis.]"

STEPH'S APARTMENT

Steph is in the kitchen area, pouring herself a glass of wine. She takes a sip, grabs the bottle and heads toward her dining/desk area. She settles in front of her computer. Quick hair flip. She's ready.

JACKSON'S APARTMENT

Jackson is asleep on a sofa. He has all manner of sci-fi toys on the floor. There are also beer bottles and a container of take-out food. The alarm on his wrist goes off. It takes him a moment to come to. No matter what has come before, Jackson always wakes up happy. But this time, he's truly pleased to have an appointment with friends. This is gonna be grand.

THE JOY'S APARTMENT

The Joy and Kimi have their stools pulled up to The Joy's computer, which is sitting on the kitchen counter. There are also two matching, elegant drinks in front of them. The Joy mans the controls. She turns to Kimi. "I'm so excited." She hits one more computer key. "And we're off!"

The Joy and Kimi can see themselves on their screen. The Joy checks her look and tries several poses with her cocktail until she hits just the right one. She holds the winning pose and at the computer she says, "Is anyone here?"

Another window pops up showing Shad and Benji in their apartment. They each have their beers and are clearly saying something at the computer, but there's no sound.

Annoyed, Kimi shakes her head. "We can't hear you."

Shad mouths something.

Kimi: "Still can't hear you."

Loudly, The Joy calls out, "Hit the unmute," which, of course, they can't hear.

Shad mouths, "What?"

Kimi: "She said you have a small dick."

Shad mouths, "What?"

Kimi says to no one, "It's like a license to kill."

Shad is finally audible, "How 'bout now?"

The Joy: "OK. We can hear you."

Shad: "Made it. Who else is here?"

Benji turns to him, "Here."

Shad shoots him a look. "I know you're here. You're here, here...with me."

Benji: "I know that."

Another window pops up. It's Steph with her wine and the large bottle of backup wine. "Hey kids."

The Joy: "Hey, lady! How you?"

Steph: "Since you asked..."

One last window pops up, cutting her off. It's Jackson. He's mixing the contents of an oversize cocktail with a tiny lightsaber. With a stately manner, he greets his friends, "People."

The Joy: "Oh, my God. The gang's back together. Yay! I missed you guys." Then turning to Kimi, "Well, not you."

Kimi: "Thanks."

Shad: "We just saw each other a week ago. This is our regular timing."

Steph: "How is everybody?"

Kimi: "Ginger peachy."

Steph: "Great." Steph was clearly just asking so she could share her own answer. "You would not believe the shit I'm dealing with at work. Is it OK that I mention work? I mean, you know. Since you're not working."

Kimi: "Sure, pick that scab."

Steph: "Super. My boss is insane. Seriously. Do you know what she asked me to do?"

Shad: "Work?"

Steph: "She asked me if I could throw some more jazz hands into a piece about miners and coronavirus...And Shad, I caught that, by the way. But jazz hands...seriously? It's like she's trapped in some 1940s fast banter movie. This is news."

Jackson: "How old are these minors?"

Steph: "Not minors, young minors. Miner miners. Coal miners out in PA.

Benji: "Jackson, nice cocktail stirrer. You find that on Tatooine?

Jackson: "Indeed, sir. The Walmart on Tatooine." Jackson reaches for something and produces a cigarette. "Anyone mind if I smoke?"

Kimi: "You do realize that none of us are in the room with you."

Jackson: "Just trying to be polite."

Shad: "You do realize that you don't smoke."

In classic James Bond fashion, Jackson lights his cigarette with the flip of a Zippo lighter. "Just something new and different to break up the day. And, I heard on the news that smokers are not getting the virus. How about that? Yay, smoking!"

Steph: "FYI, I wasn't done telling you about work. Do you know how many people in this country think that coronavirus is a conspiracy?

Jackson: "Is it?"

On the screen with Shad and Benji, the gang can see the dog jump up on Benji's lap. The Joy greets him. "Oh, Douglas. Look at you. Who's a good boy? Who's such a handsome boy?

Benji: "His name is Fluffers."

The Joy: "No, that's Douglas."

Benji: "He's Fluffers now."

Everyone looks rather confused. Shad shakes his head. "Long story." He then quickly changes the subject. "Hey, what are we all drinking?"

Benji, the only one not still confused about the dog, chimes in. "Beer."

The Joy: "I made Vodka Stingers! Like from the Broadway musical *Company*." She turns to Kimi and in her most mannered voice asks, "Kimi, are you enjoying your Vodka Stinger?"

Kimi: "It's divine."

The Joy raises her glass to Kimi, "Cheers to me, girl." Kimi just looks at her. The Joy re-raises her glass. "Don't leave me hangin'." Kimi reluctantly lifts her glass but doesn't move it to The Joy's. The Joy clinks her glass on Kimi's, "Cheers!" She then sings from *Company*, "Another Vodka Stinger!" She takes a sip. "Wow, that's good!"

Steph: "I've got wine, straight up." Steph takes a sip from the bottle.

Jackson: "I'm enjoying a lovely sloe gin fizz. Remember in high school when we got sick on these at that rager behind Shad's house?"

Shad: "Ah, memories."

Kimi: "Hard to forget the night I first questioned my sexuality."

With compassion, The Joy asks, "That's when you thought you might be gay?"

Kimi: "No, that's when I thought I might be a man."

Jackson: "And Shad had to explain to his dad the next day why his tulips all died overnight."

Shad: "I left out the part about ritual vomiting."

Jackson: "Smart move."

Shad: "Wasn't feeling so smart at the time. I think I out-vomited everyone...God, I love a win."

Benji raises his eyebrows and says, "Hey Steph, remember we made out that night?"

The Joy: "You didn't!"

Steph: "We didn't."

Benji: "We didn't?"

Steph: "Absolutely not."

Benji: "Bummer."

Jackson: "No, that was me."

The Joy: "You didn't!"

Steph: "Can we stop this?"

Kimi: "I'd rather not."

Shad: "Well, I know it wasn't me, I was too busy being the bottomless fountain of chunks...Hey Jackson. How you holding up over there? I mean, you need a hand with anything?"

Jackson: "No. Why?"

Shad: "Just that, you know, you're not working and..."

The Joy: "You're not..." she makes air quotes, "working. Nudge, nudge. Wink, wink."

Jackson: "I'm great. Really. I have a superior dwelling." Jackson turns his computer to show his digs. For the first time, everyone sees where Jackson lives. It's a goddamn palace of a Park Avenue apartment.

Shad is concerned, "Dude, whose apartment did you break into?"

Kimi: "Jackson, get the F out of there, now!"

Jackson: "Children. Chillax."

Excitedly, The Joy jumps in. "Oh, that's my word. *I* say 'Chillax.'"

Jackson: "This is my folks' place. They're stuck in the UAE for who knows how long. They're fine with me crashing here. Shit. Just don't tell them I was smoking. Do you think they have cameras?"

Kimi turns to The Joy. "Why the hell am I staying with you?"

Steph: "Well, there's an interesting turn of events."

Shad: "Damn!"

Benji: "Do you have a dog run?"

Jackson: "Perhaps. I can ask the guard. Jeffery, the day man, would know. Hey, does anyone need their shoes polished? We have a guy in the lobby."

Kim: "Of course, you do."

Shad: "Dude, did your parents always have a crap-ton of money? Like, when we were in school, I don't remember your house being any nicer than...wait, I never saw your house. But you drove that piece of shit Nova. Who drives a Nova?

Jackson: "My parents always said people act differently towards you when they know you have money. And that we shouldn't act like we think we're better than anyone else."

Shad: "You shouldn't *act* like it. But did you think it?"

Steph: "Listen, kids. I hate to break up the party, but I have to run. Janis needs—*needs*—copy to her ASAP."

The Joy: "Hey, wait. Wait. First, we have to do a cheers. Cheers, everybody! To us!"

They all raise their glasses and speak over each other, "Cheers."

"To us."

"Cheers."

"Cheers." They drink.

The Joy: "This was so great. Same time next week?"

Kimi: "Let me check my schedule." She looks around the room. "Hey, look at that. I have nowhere else to be."

Jackson: "Me either."

Shad: "In."

Benji: "We'll be here." He turns to the dog, "Won't we, Fluffers?" Fluffers barks. "Daddy loves you."

Steph: "I'll do my best. No promises."

The Joy: "Oh, you'll be there. Okay, coronavirus lockdown week one, in the books. We are signing off. Bye, guys. Cheers!"

Steph: "Bye." Steph's window bleeps and goes black.

Shad waves. Benji waves and helps Fluffers wave, then their window goes black.

Jackson: "Till next time." Jackson's window goes black.

The Joy turns to Kim, "That went well."

Kimi flatly, "Very well."

The Joy kisses Kimi's forehead and their window goes black.

THE DOG DAYS

THE JOY'S APARTMENT

Kimi yanks back her curtain and storms into the living room. "How am I supposed to think?" She's dressed in her usual casual/industrial day-wear, plus she's sporting slippers that look like dog paws and a light blue surgical mask.

The Joy, whose hair is now a bluish-blond, is on the sofa snipping at her bangs with a pair of pro clippers. "Why do you insist on wearing a mask inside?"

"Oh, I don't know. Because I'm living with Corona Carrie?"

"Oh, pet names! Fun. But I'd rather just be Carrie."

Kimi ignores that. She's getting better at looking past The Joy's madness when she has something she'd rather complain about. "Have you seen that line for the market? Every day. All day. Right below the window. Yap. Yap. Yap. Yap. I can't think. And have you listened to them?"

"Well I..."

Kimi doesn't wait for an actual answer. It would only get in the way of her rant and she wants to rant. She uses whiny voices to imitate the different people outside her window. "You're not standing far enough away from me. I'm anemic. I'm more susceptible. Waanh!" "They were out of Peet's coffee. I had to buy Chock Full o' Nuts. Waanh!" "I have to do Pilates at home now and I just can't get as motivated without Tanya. Waanh!" "My kids' tutor got sick. I can't teach them geometry. What's a rhombus? Who can tell me what a rhombus is? Can't my kids get to college without a rhombus? Waanh!" Back in her own voice, "What a bunch of fucking crybabies. How do these idiots get dressed in the morning? I think I hate people."

The Joy makes a small "Tsk," clicking her tongue behind her teeth, then says, "You know, that gal, Promise, from my book club..." The Joy often "Tsks" before she speaks, but this was the final straw.

Kimi, now fixated on the mouth noise, has a hyper reaction to the little sound. "That!!!"

"What that?"

"That! That sound you make!"

"I have a sound?"

"You 'Tsk' before you talk. I never noticed it. Or I did, but not this much. Now I can't hear anything but your fucking speech pathology."

"I could put on some ABBA. If I hear "Waterloo," I can't think of anything else for days."

With the instant realization that she will now have "Waterloo" stuck in her head for the rest of the day, Kimi says flatly, "You suck."

SHAD & BENJI'S APARTMENT

Benji is in the kitchen. He's wearing what is now his in-house look: long shorts, some sci-fi T and slippers. He has a large glass bowl filled with water and a big blob, which he's kneading. Benji leans forward and speaks to it softly. "Okay, you. I'm going to feed you every day and you're going to grow big and strong for me." He gets a towel and lays it lovingly over the bowl, then carefully puts the bowl in a corner of the counter.

Fluffers comes into the kitchen and looks up at Benji. Benji leans down to pet him. "It's OK, boy. I still love you."

JACKSON'S APARTMENT/HALLWAY

Back to the hallway. Jackson has a tool belt on that's empty except for a hammer. He also has a few nails in his mouth and a cigarette behind his ear. He's ready for this. He gets on a step stool, takes a nail from his mouth and, after checking to make sure everything is just where he wants it, hammers the nail in. He then gets a round clock and hangs it on the nail. After admiring his work, he's ready to try again.

Jackson removes the tool belt and puts it and the step stool into a closet. He then returns to the hall with his computer. He goes to the *American Ninja Warrior* Fan page on YouTube and turns the volume up. Next, he watches the second hand on his new wall clock waiting for just the right moment. Wait for it...Wait for it...Now! He jumps up and braces himself off the ground with his hands and feet jammed against the hallway walls. Here we go.

SHAD & BENJI'S APARTMENT/SHAD'S BEDROOM

Shad's at his desk, with his computer open. Again, he's dressed for work from the waist up and sporting an underwear party from the waist down. He looks at his watch. It's time. Damn, he hates these group calls. He clicks the conference call link and waits. Two of his team are already on the call. Shad greets them, "Hey, all."

Sandra is there looking like she's about to get a tooth drilled. She quietly responds, "Hey, Shad." Collin, the other guy on the call just does the head nod. They all sit waiting for the boss and their other team members to join. No one says anything for fear of being the one talking when Max gets on, therefore making them the focus of his attentions. Minutes go by.

Finally, another window comes up. It's...Christopher. Everyone gives a sigh of relief. Collin quietly addresses him. "Christopher, dude, you're pushing it."

Max's window comes on the call, "Pushing what? What is Christopher pushing?" There's a long silence.

Christopher tries, "Commodities?"

Apparently, that was the wrong answer. Max goes off for a good ten minutes on why they're putting supply-chain stocks before all else. Commodities is just a hedge. The team once again gets to hear about how crucial supply chains were in all the major wars ever fought. Max is a war buff. He does know his shit, but how many times can you hear it and pretend that it all sounds fresh and revelatory?

Max comes to the end of his rant. "You all got that, right?" There are low-level agreements from the team. Max switches to the always-popular topic of the team's call volume. "So how many calls have we made today? Anyone? Bueller? Bueller?" Max laughs to himself.

Sandra is about to say something when her young son runs into her room and starts pulling on her arm. She tries to nudge the boy away, while smiling uncomfortably at her computer.

Christopher steps up saying, "I started with Mr. Walsh and..."

"Walsh? John Walsh?" Max interrupts. "That's a weenie call. Isn't he your mother's cousin or some such shit? Did you make any real calls? Any calls to anyone where blood wasn't involved? The time is at hand, people. This is what we've all been waiting for. It's the Rubber Duck Rally! You just had a front row seat to the biggest rally ever! Ever! We need to be on the phones. I don't want to hear about your emails. I don't want to hear about your texts. I want phone calls. We need to make personal contact here, because rubber duckies are gonna do what rubber duckies do. And what is that? Someone answer me or I'm going to go ballistic. What do rubber duckies do?"

Everyone knows the answer, but by Max going big, the team recoils and goes small. All these young guns who, by comparison to their friends, are A-types, are cowed by Max's type A-plus. Shad's now tarnished and can't take it anymore. He decides to cowboy up. As if reciting military procedure, he says, "Rubber ducks can't take the pressure of being pulled underwater forever, so they finally shoot way up, then they bounce a little lower each time until they settle."

Max, "Thank you, Jesus! Someone listened. There is a god."

Shad feels good about his choice to not be Max's punching bag. He thinks fortune favors the bold. Or does it?

Max says, "Shad, stand up. Take a well-deserved bow."

Shad's taken aback. "Excuse me?"

"You heard me. Stand up. Bow."

"That's okay."

"Take a goddamn bow, Shad." Shad slowly rises letting the team see that he's in his boxer/briefs. Not good.

Max booms, "Is that how a New York financial animal dresses to convince his clients that he knows how to set them up for financial success? Can you possibly feel like you are in control when this is how you show up? You're in your goddamn underwear! OK. I gotta know. Everyone. I want all of you to stand up. Right now. On your feet." The team is reluctant. Without raising his voice, Max asserts, "Stand the F up!"

The rest of the team slowly stands up. They are all dressed business on top, pajama party on the bottom.

SHAD & BENJI'S APARTMENT

Benji is on the sofa, again, watching the news. There's a guy in Texas standing by his truck, wearing a red, white and blue T-shirt who doesn't want his rights taken away. He's an American, damn it. Cut to a woman at a lectern talking about how it's too hard to breathe in a mask. She has a right to air. It says so in the Bible. Cut to a line of nurses getting confronted outside of a clinic by angry people with signs that read, "You're Killing America." Benji clicks off the TV and sits in silence for a while. Fluffers jumps up on his lap and looks back and forth from Benji to the TV.

After a few minutes, Benji turns the TV back on. People are standing in line outside of a Walmart. There's a run on all essentials. Cut to shots of empty shelves. Cut to people yelling at a grocery store owner. Benji starts shaking. This is so disturbing. He can feel a spiral coming on.

To save himself, he switches away from the news and puts on a horror movie. Some guy is running with a giant power tool. He's chasing a gal towards the water. Right before he gets her, a huge gator rises out of the river and bites Mr. Power Tool in half. Blood and guts spray everywhere, including on to the gal who was about to die. Benji can feel himself slowly calming down.

THE JOY'S APARTMENT

The Joy is at her front door escorting a woman and her daughter out. The mother, Beatrice, has an eclectic, moneyed vibe. Her child just has a child vibe. Both guests look like they've been freshly quaffed. They all quietly look at Kimi's closed curtain. It's safe. Beatrice hands The Joy a rolled up bill and then rethinks it saying in a hushed voice, "Oh, do you take cash or are we not touching money right now?"

The Joy thinks about this and says, "You're right. Can you Venmo me the tip?"

"Sure thing."

"Super. Okay, I have you both down for one month from now."

"You're the best."

"No, you."

The Joy and Beatrice hug and Beatrice and her daughter leave. The Joy shuts the door after them thinking, "COVID's not so bad, really."

KIMI'S CORNER

Kimi's in her new standard position as one with the La-Z-Boy. She hears the front door close and shakes her head. Idiots.

She has her computer on her lap and notepads all around. She's looking over web pages for different face masks and making notes, freehand. She types in, "Flower face masks." Damn. More than she thought there would be. Way more than the last time she looked. But maybe the designs suck. Hmm, most do suck. That's good. A few are decent. She starts making sketches on her note pad. Does she like that sketch? No. She's forcing it. She switches to the business side of things. What are people charging? More notes. She then looks up the cost for printing masks to see what kind of margin there is. It looks like she can have masks printed for just under four dollars apiece. And sell them for, what? Fourteen? Could she get more? Maybe, if there was something truly special about them.

She thinks to herself, "I thought I was smarter than this. People are making money all over the place. What's wrong with me? Why can't I see the path to success? What the fuck is wrong with me?"

Needing a break, she goes to the news on YouTube. Seems that the infection and death rates are still rising and New York is still one of the hot spots in the U.S. "Motherfucker." Now she needs a break from her break.

She puts everything aside and peers out of her privacy curtain. No Joy in sight. Kimi heads to the back window. She's got her technique down for traversing the windowsill juju and getting onto the fire escape. She sits and stares blankly. After a while she notices clarinet music and looks around. Some of her regulars are out. Mr. Clarinet has gotten a little better. Oh, wait. No. He's not.

Kimi's phone vibrates and she sees that it's a text from Carmen, reading, "Hey kiddo. Any better? [Question face emoji]" Kimi pockets her phone and goes back to staring.

STEPH'S APARTMENT

Steph, wearing a mask, stands back as two large men, also wearing masks that are not as cute as hers, drag a large box through her entry hall. The box is marked, "Peloton." She points to a corner by her window wall. "Can you put it over there, by the big plant?" They shuffle their way over. "And maybe pick it up instead of dragging it?" The men shake their heads, but do their best to pick up the box. They deal with a lot of New York women. They place the box in the corner.

Large Man #1 looks to Steph. "This work?"

Not totally pleased, Steph thinks, "Further to the right would be better." The men nudge the box over a bit.

The same large man looks to her again, "Now?"

Still not pleased, Steph settles." Fine." Fine never really means fine. But the men start heading to the door.

Steph calls out, "Wait!" The men look back to her. "Aren't you going to take it out of the box?"

Large Man #1 explains, "Lady, look. We drive the truck. We unload the truck. We get back in said truck."

Surprised by the phrasing, Steph retorts, "Said truck? We're very formal, are we not?"

Just as Large Man #1 is about to counter retort, Large Man #2 spots a picture of Steph on a wall with David Muir. He looks around and sees her with other celebs in and out of the news. "Wait, you're that chick from the news—the one with the hair."

"Most of us have hair. It's kind of a thing."

Large Man #2 thinks. Then, "I got that. That's funny."

"Could you tell my mother? She doesn't think I'm funny."

Large Man #2 pulls his cell out. "Can I get a picture...for my kids?" Steph acquiesces and moves behind him. Not too close.

As he frames and reframes the selfie, Steph gets impatient. "So your kids are big news fans?"

"Nah, it's for me." He snaps the picture. Nice moment.

Large Man #1 puts his hands in his pockets. "So you bein' on the news and all, you can afford to tip. I mean, you bein 'on the news and all."

Steph's cell rings. It's her mother. She turns to the large men, "I have to take this."

Large Man #1 is unsurprised. "Of course, you do."

ZOOM

THE JOY'S APARTMENT

The Joy is sitting on a bar stool at her kitchen counter. Her computer is open and two drinks sit next to it. She calls out, "Kimi? Kimi Girl? It's time to Zoom!"

Kimi comes out from behind her curtain wearing a mask. The Joy looks over. "Still?"

Kimi hops on a bar stool. "Let's see. You're seeing all kinds of people. Touchin 'all kinds of shit. Receiving all kinds of *packages*. We're gonna be sitting this close. Yeah, still."

Kimi reaches for one of the cocktails and The Joy grabs. "I don't think that's safe. I'm touching all kinds of shit...and licking it." She licks the entire rim of both cocktails.

The two don't realize that while they're arguing, the rest of the gang has joined the video call and seen their domestic issues play out.

Steph swirls the wine in her glass. "Should we come back another time?"

The Joy and Kimi turn to the computer. The gang waves. The Joy tries to cover, "Hey guys. It's fine. We were just sharing germs. Right, roomie?" Kimi huffs.

Jackson is holding himself propped up off the ground in his hallway. "Now, ladies. Play nice. You need each other."

Shad looks quizzically at Jackson. He can't get close enough to his screen to confirm to himself what he's seeing. "Are you...in the air?"

Jackson: "I'm setting a record."

Shad: "Excuse what?"

Jackson reaches for a drink from a new shelf up high on the hallway wall, takes a sip, replaces it. "I'm setting a record, friends. Longest time off the ground holding oneself wedged between two walls. I don't want to have nothing to show for my time in lock down. I'm setting a world record."

Benji: "Bro, that's so cool."

Steph: "And what's the old record for holding oneself wedged?"

Jackson thinks for a moment. "You know, I don't know. I never thought to look."

Benji grabs his phone. "Hold on. I'll look it up." There's silence as Benji checks his phone. "No." He keeps checking. "No." He checks some more. The group silently drinks their respective drinks. "I'm not finding anything."

Jackson: "Did you try self-supporting?"

Benji tries. "Nothing."

Steph: "Did you try self-wedging?

Kimi: "That's only funny once."

Benji: "I'm not seeing anything. I don't think there is a record for...whatever it is that you're doing."

The Joy: "Wait. Wait. Great news. Jackson, how long have you been up there?"

Jackson looks at his wall clock. "Five hours and about...twenty-five minutes."

The Joy: "We have a new world record! Longest wall wedgy. Five hours, twenty-five minutes. You can come down now."

Jackson reaches for his cocktail and poses. "Quick, someone take a screen shot!"

Benji: "So let it be done...Got it."

With that, Jackson takes another sip, jumps down and does a grand dismount bow. "I'm glad you all could be a part of this historic occasion." Everyone applauds. Jackson's legs are a bit wobbly, but he can stand. "I thank you all."

Benji: "And now, I have something that we can all be a part of." He leaves frame. Shad shrugs to the group, indicating he has no idea what's in store. Benji returns with his towel-covered, glass bowl.

He pulls back the towel and Shad is hit in the face with a smell. He recoils. "What that smell, man?"

The Joy: "Ever notice that nothing good ever follows the phrase, *What's that smell?*"

Benji:" It's my sourdough starter. It's a living thing. I feed it daily. I think you guys should all do it. It'll be like having a pet. I've named mine Douglas."

Shad: "Douglas? Really?"

Benji: "Well, the name became available."

The Joy: "I like it. I was thinking of getting another pet, but this is better. It's like a pet you can eat!"

Kimi: "I'm not taking on another mouth to feed."

Steph: "Seriously, I don't need another obligation."

Benji: "Come on. It'll be fun. You can all do it. Yeast is in the air."

Kimi: "Isn't that the tagline for a douche?"

Benji ignores her and presses on. "And someday our sourdough kids can all have a play date."

Kimi: "I thought they were pets. I'm not ready for kids. Just ask my mother."

Benji gives his best pathetic face. "Come on. Please. For me."

Jackson: "I'm ready for a new challenge. What do I do?"

Benji's delighted with having a taker. "Yes. You're all gonna love this. I'll text you guys everything you need to know. If you have any questions, just ask me. I know being a new parent can be daunting. But you're gonna be great."

Shad: "Can't I just co-parent?"

Benji: "Don't take this as a criticism of what I believe your parenting skills will be someday, but no."

Kimi: "Ouch."

Steph: "If you'll all excuse me for I moment, I have to go to the little announcer's booth." She gets up and heads to her large handbag on her kitchen counter.

Shad: "That reminds me. Who here has tried to buy toilet paper?" Shad watches Steph in the distance pull a roll of toilet paper from her bag and head out of frame. "What the hell?"

The Joy: "I know. There's like a run on pooping." She thinks for a moment. "No. Wait. It's like a run on the runs. Get it?"

 Shad: "Did you see that? Did anyone see that?"

Jackson: "What are you talking about?"

Shad: "That roll of paper Steph just pulled out of her bag. Just there. It wasn't in a package. You didn't see it? Tell me someone saw it."

Kimi: "Wow, you need to get out."

Shad: "I'm not going crazy. I think she's pinching paper." There's no response. "Pinching... Stealing. She's got black market toilet paper."

Steph returns to frame.

Shad: "Aha!" There's silence. He tries again. "Aha!"

Steph looks at everyone. "Oh, was that for me?"

Shad: "Oh, yes. That was for you, missy."

Steph: "Missy?"

Kimi: "Is it me or has Shad gone back to 1945?"

Shad: "I saw you pull a roll of toilet paper out of your bag. It wasn't from the market, was it? Where'd you get it?" Steph doesn't answer. "You stole it. From work. Didn't you?"

Steph: "What if I did?"

Shad: "The rest of us are crinkling up newspaper to wipe, getting the obituaries on our butts and having to shower it off."

The Joy raises her hand. "I'm not doing that."

Benji: "Not it."

Shad: "A little support here, please. One of our own is breaking ranks. You're using your position of privilege for personal gain. *J'accuse!*"

Jackson: "I enjoy a nice bidet, personally, and this is probably the wrong time to say that my doorman has a bidet connection."

Steph: "Look. I'm a Jewish girl from Jersey. We wipe a lot. It's in our culture."

With extra sarcasm, Kimi says, "Never saw that coming."

Shad changes his focus to Jackson. "You have a connection?"

Steph: "Aha! *J'accuse!* I'm a horrible person, but when something can benefit you, it's OK?"

Shad: "Yes."

Steph: "Look, fella, I'm putting my life on the line for this city. The least I could get in return is the ability to clean up down there! You want the news, then let me wipe, goddamn it."

Silence.

The Joy: "Well, I feel like we accomplished a lot this week."

Kimi: "Oh, we're not done."

The Joy: "You have something you'd like to share with the group?"

Kimi: "I do."

The Joy: "You have the floor."

Kimi: "I know that some of us don't feel like they need to take the appropriate precautions against the virus." They all know who she means. "But, for those of us who would like to live through this and have the opportunity to kill ourselves properly, with drugs and alcohol, have you thought about getting a face mask with, let's say, flair? Perhaps a mask that's more of an accessory?"

Steph: "What do you have in mind?"

Defensively, The Joy says, "Some of us like accessories."

"Hold on." Kimi jumps off her stool and scoots to her corner to get something. The group watches as the curtain gets pulled back.

Shad: "Hey, are those the new digs?"

Steph: "Oh, yeah. Let's see. Give us the tour."

The Joy picks up her computer and starts walking with it to Kimi's corner. "Come with me. I'll give you the grand tour."

Kimi grabs a note pad, then sees The Joy coming her way. "What? No. My chair's not made...Really? Shit. Fine. Look. Fine." She gestures to different parts of her corner and speaks to the group. "Bedroom slash office zone, dressing zone, food zone, front door." She abruptly closes the curtain, putting a definitive end to the tour. She walks The Joy back to the kitchen counter.

Shad: "Love what you've done with the place. Really."

Kimi: "For that, smart guy, you're going to be my first customer. Now, I want to review my business plan. I emailed you all a copy."

Steph: "I, uh, really need to go. Listen, I'll review it ASAP and get back to you with notes. I'm sure it's great."

Jackson: "I'll get to it tomorrow right after my 3 p.m. cos-play."

Benji: "Are we leaving?"

Shad: "While the getting's good. 'Bye, all. Next time."

The Joy raises her glass, "Cheers everyone! Love you all."

Everyone overtalks their goodbyes and all the screens go black. Kimi sits dejected with her notepad on her lap.

THE BRIDE OF DOG DAYS

SHAD & BENJI'S APARTMENT/SHAD'S BEDROOM

Shad's laying on his bed wearing a NYC Marathon T-shirt that still shows the remnants of sweat from a recent workout. His treadmill is out from under the bed and set up in the narrow alley between bed and wall. He stares at the ceiling, thinking about life. "Why am I not more assertive? Why do I let Max cow me? I'm pathetic. I should leave. Just say, fuck it, I'm out." He thinks for a while on how great it would be to leave his job. Maybe start something small of his own. Bring Collin and Christopher with him. Not Sandra. No one with young kids. They're too distracting. Then his mind jumps to romance. "I wonder if Eva would give me another shot. Bet she'd like to go out with a man with his own firm? Someone who's his own man."

On that thought, Shad's hand travels down his chest and he reaches for himself. It's been a while. "Hello, Mr. Lucky." Shad begins to make himself feel better when...He hears a rhythmic banging from outside his room. Motherfucker. He calls out, "I can hear you!" The banging stops abruptly.

JACKSON'S APARTMENT

On the huge-screen TV in the dark entertainment room, Jackson is watching *American Ninja Warrior* reruns. As each contestant goes, Jackson roots for their success. Why not? When he listens to the next contestant's backstory he imagines himself in the competition. What would his story sound like? He certainly doesn't have a hard-luck story to share and he and everyone in his family are perfectly healthy. His grandparents are still alive and all of his great grandparents died of old age. Really old age. What would make him stand out? He thinks to himself, "What if he helped a lot of people? What if I...hmm. I don't know. Who can I help? Strangers or friends?" He's stumped but has every confidence in himself that he can solve this new puzzle. "Until then..."

Jackson gets up and starts positioning ottomans at just the right distance apart to mimic the beginning of the *Ninja Warrior* obstacle course. That looks right. He looks back at the TV. No, they need to be a little farther apart. He makes the needed adjustments, then readies himself. He takes a pass at leaping from ottoman to ottoman. Flawless. He raises his hands and announces to no one, "Oh, my God. Jackson Asghar, a walk-on, just blew this course up! Remember that name. Jackson Asghar. We expect to see a lot of great things from this man."

STEPH'S APARTMENT

It's early morning and Steph is in the front by the window wall on her new Peloton bike. She makes working up a sweat look good. The trainer on her bike says, "Come on. You can do this. Finish strong." Steph digs in and does her last miles in the same time as her first mile, which was twenty-five miles ago. She raises her arms in triumph. "Yes!" Wow, she's whipped, but she likes it.

She stares out her window for a moment, thinking about herself crossing a finish line at Alpe d'Huez in France to a cheering crowd. After basking in her victory, she looks at her watch. Shit. She's gotta get moving. Is there any way she could just pull her hair back and pass on a shower? She goes to the mirror in her bedroom and pulls her hair back. Doing this, she's able to get a whiff from under her arm. To the showers, lady.

SHAD & BENJI'S APARTMENT

Benji is at the kitchen sink with his bowl of sourdough. He arranges everything on the counter just so and pulls out his phone. He's about to snap a pic, but decides to move a card closer to the bowl. The card reads, "Douglas, One Week Old." He's happier now and takes the picture. After adjusting the color and saturation, he texts the pic to the group with the caption, "My boy."

Then he sends another text reading, "Would love to see pics of your kids." He leans against the fridge and beams over his son.

JACKSON'S APARTMENT

Jackson is hanging metal rings on chains from the ceiling, the kind of metal rings you'd see on *American Ninja Warrior*, when suddenly he gets a text from Benji. He sees the picture and smiles.

To the kitchen. He crosses his expansive apartment and heads to a large glass bowl on the counter with a towel over it. He snaps a picture and shoots it back on the text thread with the message, "Meet Shylow."

KIMI'S CORNER

From her usual position, Kimi is in the middle of deciding which print-on-demand provider she's going to go with. The one that's a better price is also limited in their ink colors. Tough choice. She ignores the first two text notifications that she hears. On the third text, she stops what she's doing and looks at her phone, thinking it could be important. She immediately rethinks that. It's probably not important. Important things aren't happening to her at the moment. She sees the thread. "Sourdough. Really? This is such nonsense." She hits the button on the La-Z-Boy, lowering her feet. She gets up, yanks open the curtain and storms out.

THE JOY'S APARTMENT

Kimi storms into the living room with her phone out. The Joy is watching the news on TV with the sound off. Kimi notices and without breaking stride, "No sound?"

"It's less depressing...Hey, there's Steph!" Then as if she hadn't seen her friend in years, notes, "She hasn't changed." To Kimi she asks, "What's up, lady?'

"Dough babies."

Kimi goes to the kitchen counter, takes a picture of a bowl full of something brown and sends it to the text thread with the caption, "Jane Doe."

The Joy gets a text and looks at her phone. "Oh, that's funny. But D-O-U-G-H would be funnier."

Kimi storms back behind her curtain.

SHAD & BENJI'S APARTMENT/BATHROOM

Shad is in his bedroom at his computer. He's dressed for the office, head to toe. He looks at the last text message and thinks, "Spelling it like 'dough' would have been funnier."

It's almost time for his team meeting. He wonders if this is going to be the time he declares, "I'm out. But before I go, let me tell you what your problem is."

No. This is probably not the time.

SHAD & BENJI'S APARTMENT

Benji is on the sofa watching *Mrs. Maisel* with Fluffers by his side and a bowl of popcorn on his lap. Shad, still dressed for work and not in a great mood, walks through and stares at him. "Is that *Mrs. Maisel*? Bro, weren't you watching that yesterday?"

Without taking his eyes off the screen, Benji says, "I'm almost done with the second season."

"And weren't you wearing that yesterday...and the day before that?"

Still focused on *Mrs. Maisel*, Benji answers, "Comedy happens in threes."

"So?" Shad starts to get sucked into what's on the screen. Without looking away he says, "What'cha eatin'?"

Silently, Benji lifts up the bowl of popcorn. Shad peers in, comes around the sofa, sits and takes a handful of the crunchy, fluffy goodness. They're both now sucked into the life of Mrs. Maisel. Shad marvels at the popcorn. "This is really good. What's in this?"

"Parmesan cheese and extra-sharp white cheddar. Oh, and a little Old Bay Seasoning."

"Genius."

They sit silently as Mrs. Maisel performs a rather blue set for her father in the Catskills. Dad is not happy, but she presses on.

Benji muses, "Did you ever notice that popcorn is the only food that you roll around on your face until it goes in the hole?"

"Genius."

At the end of the episode, the spell is broken. Benji looks up. "Don't you have to work?"

"This is way better. Wanna watch the next one?"

STEPH'S APARTMENT

Steph is dressed for work. She's staring out her window while taking a video call on her cell with Janis. Man, Janis just looks worse by the minute. She's really letting herself go.

Janis, not sounding very business-like, shares "I just needed a friendly ear, you know?"

Steph is visibly uncomfortable with her boss using her as a therapist, but doesn't feel she has the latitude to say so. "Oh, yeah. Sure."

Janis dives in. "Oh, my God! My girlfriend. Margaret. She's making me crazy. I mean, I thought it just made sense that we move in together, you know, with the virus. Otherwise, when would we see each other? Right?"

"Right."

"So I'm having her quarantine for two weeks in the spare bedroom. I mean, that's just smart procedure. And now, Margaret's mad because I'm not sending her the food she likes to eat. Just the food *I* like to eat."

Confused, Steph asks, "I'm sorry. And what do you mean by, sending her food?"

"I leave it on a tray at her door. Then I knock and run."

Steph wonders if she heard that right. "So like in solitary?"

"Exactly. And I'm ordering food from some great places. Jeffrey's, The Copper Vessel, 33's... all on my dime. And she's mad. Do you believe that?"

No safe answer here. Steph just replies with a, "Mmm."

"I mean, this pandemic was going to be so great for our relationship and now..." There's a beep on Steph's cell.

Janis is put out." What is that? Is that you?"

"Yeah. I have an incoming call." Steph sees that it's her mother. "Listen, I have to take this."

"Go ahead...I can hold."

Not exactly what Steph wanted to hear. She takes a deep breath, centers herself and switches over to her mother. "Yeah, Mom."

Ida is being Ida. "That's how you greet your mother?"

"Sorry. I'm on another call with work."

"Well, I won't bother you. It's just that your aunt is mailing you a challah and she wants to know if she should send it to your apartment or to your work."

"She's sending me a challah?"

"Yes. Should she send it to your apartment or to your work?"

"Why is she sending me a challah? I live in New York City. This town is lousy with challah. You can't swing a dead cat without hitting a challah."

"Oh, honey, don't do that."

"No. I mean…"

"Your aunt and her friends have been making these challahs special for years. Everyone loves them. There was an article about them in the Philadelphia Inquirer. The mayor got one…without raisins. It's a pretty big deal." Ida slips into guilt mode. "But if you want me to tell Jean that you wouldn't appreciate it…"

Steph knows it'll be easier to just let this happen. "No. No. It'll be great. I'd love to get one. Tell Jean she can send it to the apartment."

"Are you sure? If she sends it to work you'll be the envy of all your co-workers. They might even want to do a news story about it. These challahs are a very big deal. I'll tell her to send it to your office."

"If you knew where you wanted her to send it, why did you ask?"

"I thought you might get it right."

Steph shakes her head, "Listen, Mom…"

"I know. I know. You have work. Go. I'll talk to you another time."

"OK. Give Dad my love."

"I will. He loves you, too. Go to work." The line clicks off.

After a moment to switch gears again, Steph says, "Janis? Are you still there?"

Oh, she's there. "Where else am I going to go?"

"You won't believe the call I just…"

Janis doesn't seem interested in hearing about Steph's world. She blurts, "This just in. Margaret wants rice pudding. Rice, fucking, pudding. Excuse me for liking tapioca. Oh, and she wants the kind without raisins. Who the hell has a raisin allergy?

Steph asks, "How does she feel about challah?"

THE JOY'S APARTMENT

Vlad, the PackageGuys guy, is leaving. He looks back and gives The Joy a wink and heads out. The Joy closes the door, still in the afterglow of receiving a package. She turns and...

"*J'accuse!*" Kimi is sitting on the sofa watching *When Sharks Attack*. The Joy nearly jumps out of her skin. "Oh, my God! You almost scared me to death. I'm banning that word. Ixnay on the J'accuse-ay. I was just getting a package."

"A package or a *package*? And was that a new hair cut?"

"It was just a trim."

"*A* trim or *some* trim?"

"Stop it. The Joy doesn't like this game either. Vlad is very responsible."

This is the first that Kimi has heard Mr. PackageGuys' name. It's like a new toy. "Vlad? As in, Vlad The Impaler? That's perfect."

The Joy has had enough. "I'm going to hang out with The Fred. He's not all judgy, like you." She heads to the bedroom calling out, "Fred! Come on, Fred."

Kimi calls after her, "You forgot the, 'The!'"

Kimi sits alone. She tries to turn back to the sharks, but there are distant voices that are pulling her attention. They're coming from outside. What now? She heads over to the front window and looks out. The line of people wearing masks and waiting to get into the market spans the length of the sidewalk. And they're all talking. Lots of loud conversations. Kimi pulls up her mask and leans out the window. A kind-looking man in a cardigan walks past the line pulling his full grocery bags in a small cart. An uptight fortyish guy calls out to him. "Hey! Hey, do they still have lemongrass?"

Cardigan Man answers, "How the fuck should I know?" He keeps walking.

The Fortyish Guy turns to the woman in line behind him and explains, "It's for my smoothies. That's not so crazy."

To the left there are two older men in line in their older-men clothes. Kimi drops in. Older Man 1 says to his friend, "My brother, Jacob, you remember, he's in Miami. In a fifty-five and over. He says no one there has left their house in weeks. They're all afraid. Sixty and over is more susceptible. Look at me. Should I be out here?"

"You know what I say?" responds Older Man 2, "Fuck it. I'm seventy-eight. *Something's* gonna kill me."

"Nothing's gonna kill you. But you know what else he said? Jacob? He said they're all runnin' around schtuppin' each other after dark."

Older Man 2 thinks about that. "That's how I want to go." They laugh. "I could go for that. Don't tell Terry."

Kimi turns her attention and listens in to the two women right below her window. They're dressed in their best Lululemon. Lemon Lady 1 poses, "If Angie wants to stifle her kid's progress, well..."

Lemon Lady 2 goes for the agreement. "I know. All those rules. It's just going to stifle them. I can already tell that Maggie is rebelling."

"I know. They're going to end up hating her. It's just so..."

Kimi calls out of her window, "Stifling?"

The ladies look up and see Kimi sitting in her window. Lemon Lady 1 calls up, "Do you mind? This is a private conversation."

Kimi yells back," Doesn't sound private. See, if it was a private conversation, I wouldn't be able to hear it."

The Lemon Ladies turn their backs to Kimi and speak in more hushed voices.

The Joy appears in the window next to Kimi. She's wearing a flowy top that's particularly colorful. "Who are you talking to?"

"I'm not talking. I'm listening."

Lemon Lady 1 turns to them and adds, "She's listening in and it's very rude."

Defending her own, The Joy snaps, "You wanna know what's rude? A shag hair cut in 2020. Why don't you just put on matching jogging suits and go back to 1983?"

Kimi can't help but laugh. "And that right there is why we're friends."

The Joy smiles and they both head back into their inner sanctuary. The Joy has an inspiration. "Want a Vodka Stinger?'

Having some of her stress relieved, at least for the moment, Kimi's in. "Sure."

JACKSON'S APARTMENT

With *Star Wars Rogue One* on the big screen in the entertainment room, Jackson hangs from two of the *Ninja Warrior*-like rings that are now secured to the ceiling. He's in a muscle shirt, the kind that costs sixty dollars, and long shorts. His cell rings and he hangs from one hand to get it. It's Benji. Jackson answers, "Talk to me."

With geeky excitement, Benji's question is more of a statement. "You're watching, right?"

"I'm watching."

"This is the best one, right?"

"Totally the best one."

They both stay on the line but say nothing as they continue watching the movie.

SHAD & BENJI'S APARTMENT

Shad is in his bedroom pacing. Like Steve McQueen in *Papillon*, he counts off his steps as he goes. Seven steps...wall. Seven good strides to get across the long way. He tries to match his foot falls each time.

Seven...Seven...Seven...Seven. Maybe this is how he'll think himself out of his career rut. He'll pace dramatically, like in the movies. Seven...Seven...Seven... He'll be totally driven. He'll turn into a financial animal. Seven...Seven...Seven... He'll not be cowed. He'll grow his base. Seven...Seven...Seven... He'll stand up to Max-a-Billion... Seven...Seven...Seven..."Fuck this."

Shad stops and sits on his bed. He thinks, "My God. I can't even commit to this tedious act. Prisoners do it. What's wrong with me?" He thinks for a long time, but comes to no actionable conclusion.

COCKTAIL NIGHT

THE JOY'S APARTMENT

The Joy and Kimi are at opposite ends of the sofa, facing each other. There are various bags of salty snacks, all of which end in the suffix "-itos," open between them. Each of them are holding a Manhattan. There's New Orleans funk playing in the background.

Kimi continues a thought. "I could never *hate* you. Well, never say never."

"Come on. Be nice to me."

"That is my nice."

The Joy takes a sip of her drink. "Mmm. This is good. I could be a bartender."

"Not a lot of call for that right now."

"I could be a virtual bartender."

Confused, but not surprised, Kimi asks, "What does that mean?"

"I don't know. Come up with something. You're the brain."

"Oh, I'm a genius. I spend my genius day sitting in my corner—correction, sitting in *your* corner, drawing face masks that no one will ever buy. Genius."

"I'll buy one."

"You never wear a mask."

"But I'd buy one." On a dime, The Joy changes the conversation to, "Hey, if we were in prison, would you want to have sex with me?"

"Wow, that's random."

"I just mean, you know, in prison, you have to make choices you may not make in gen-pop."

Kimi corrects her, "First of all, gen-pop is still in prison. It's just not in solitary or otherwise separated from the general prison population."

"Wow. Why do you know so much about prison? Is there something you want to tell me?"

"Not yet."

The Joy muses, "I just wonder if women would find me attractive...should something happen."

"I just don't know where you're going with this."

"Just fishing for compliments."

"Well then. You have a pretty mouth."

The Joy is completely flattered by this and basks in the moment. "How are things with you and Carmen?"

Bad topic. Kimi rolls her eyes. "Please."

"What?"

Rant time. Kimi dives in. "Carmen's all put out that I don't want to talk to her about my *feeeelings*. She's always all, 'How do you *feeeel* about this. How do you *feeeel* about that? I never know how you *feeeel*.' Jesus Christ! I *feeeel* like I shouldn't have to talk about that shit. And this, my friend is the down side of dating women. Too many feelings. Too much, 'What did you mean when you said that?' Guys don't do that shit. A guy says something, you know what he means? Exactly what he just fucking said."

Realizing that she's hit a vein, The Joy changes it up. "Wow. Okay then. Which one of the guys would you sleep with?"

"What guys?"

"You know. Our guys. Shad, Benji and Jackson."

"Those are my guy choices? I think I'm gonna need a refill." Kimi holds up her empty glass.

The Joy happily pops up, grabs it and heads for the kitchen. She goes to wash out the glasses and realizes she's out of dish soap. "Shit. We're out of soap."

Kimi leaps to her feet, rushes to her corner and returns with two fresh bottles of dish soap, one lemon scent, one summer breeze scent, and a new sponge. "Here you go."

"Look at that. You travel with cleaning supplies."

"You don't?" Kimi returns to the sofa.

The Joy carefully fixes the new drinks. "You know, we should get Steph in on this. Call her up."

Kimi makes a face, like calling Steph would be so much work. The Joy talks to her like she's talking to a child. "Just do it."

Kimi calls Steph. It rings several times. "She's not picking up."

Just then, Steph picks up. "Hey. What's up?"

The Joy calls out, "Put her on speaker." Kimi does as told. The Joy calls out again, "Hey, lady! We're having in important conversation. Grab a drink and join us."

"Too late. Already have one. I believe my wine glass has now become an extension of my hand."

The Joy heads back to the sofa with the refreshed, lovely looking drinks. She could be a bartender. "You're so funny." She then shakes her head to Kimi, indicating that she doesn't really think that Steph is funny. She says aloud, "Put Steph on video."

Steph resists, "Oh, no. I look like shit."

Suddenly forceful, The Joy barks, "Do it."

Kimi hits video and Steph comes on Kimi's cell. "That's you looking like shit? Fuck you."

"Nice to see you, too."

Kimi asks, but not really, "Couldn't you at least put a piece of parsley in your teeth?"

"Do I need this?"

The Joy jumps in to save the call." Hey, lady. We were launching an important conversation and wanted your input."

"Sorry. I'm all virused out."

"Ugh. No. No virus talk. Kimi, take your mask off. It just serves as a reminder."

"I will not."

"Fine. Whatever." The Joy hopes for better things from her new party member. "So Steph, here's the thing. Who would you sleep with, Shad, Benji or Jackson? Unless you've already done the deed, in which case, tell us which one?"

Steph is taken a back, but only for a moment. "Oh, this is important. Jackson."

Kimi: "Really?"

Steph: "Why is that a surprise. He's hot."

Kimi: "He's also Middle Eastern. Isn't that against the laws of kosher?"

"I didn't say I'd marry him." Steph considers that scenario playing out. "Could you imagine? My parents would shit. It would be like bringing home the ultimate bad boy."

The Joy: "Wouldn't that be Jesus?"

Kimi: "You lost me...again."

The Joy: "Well, Jesus is the ultimate Jewish bad boy. Right? It's like he said, 'Hey, Mom and Dad, I won't be home for Passover. I'm gonna hang with my posse and start a new religion.'"

Steph: "You've clearly given this some thought."

The Joy: "I've had time on my hands."

Steph: "OK, your turn. Which one would you sleep with?"

The Joy: "For me it's less about which one and more about who first. It's like planning a meal. Like, I think I'd start with Benji, cause he'd be a bit of a freak, but sweet. Appetizer. Then Shad would be like the sorbet. Real neutral, standard stuff. Then I'd finish with Jackson, cause that could get super freaky and athletic, you know? Main course." She considers her plan. "Yeah, that works."

Steph: "You *have* had time on your hands."

Kimi: "Are they all going to visit you in one night, like in *A Christmas Carol*?"

The Joy considers this. Interesting. "I didn't think about splitting them up."

Steph: "I wonder what the guys talk about without us."

Kimi: "Sandwiches."

SHAD & BENJI'S APARTMENT

Benji and Shad are in the kitchen. Benji, who's still in his new favorite anime shirt, has just given Shad a large, drippy cheesesteak. "Just try it."

Shad has to figure out how he's going to attack this monster. He finally gets his head at just the right angle for a large bite. Benji stares at him while he chews. He needs to know.

Shad reviews his bite." That's damn close, brother."

Benji's disappointed with his near-hit. "What am I missing?"

"I think it's just the bread. That Atlantic City bread...God, I'd love a sandwich from the White House right now...Not that this is bad." Shad steals another bite before Benji can get the sandwich back.

Benji cuts the sandwich and puts half of it on a plate for Shad. "OK, three best sandwiches of all time...go."

"Number one. White House cheesesteak, fried onions and mushrooms..."

Benji protests, "No mushrooms."

"This is my list."

"Let's get Jackson in on this. He'll back me up."

Shad, sure that he'll get support on this important matter, offers, "Fine. Call Jackson." He grabs a beer for each of them and they settle on the sofa.

THE JOY'S APARTMENT

The Joy and Kimi are still on the call with Steph. All three are now completely in the bag. The salty snacks have been ravaged. Steph pulls a box out from under her couch. It's filled with sugary treats. She opens a foil pack of strawberry Pop-Tarts.

The Joy is aghast, "Oh, no. How can you eat the ones without the frosting?"

"I look at unfrosted Pop-Tarts as a diet snack. But just in case..." Steph takes her phone and her Pop-Tarts over to her Peloton bike, gets on and starts pedaling. "That should do it."

Kimi: "You think?"

Steph: "Nah. I just like how the seat feels."

They all laugh until The Joy gets completely serious. "Okay, Kimi, spill it. You're in prison..."

Kimi: "Again?"

The Joy: "No, wait. Wait. This is important. You're in prison, and Steph and I are your cellmates. Who do you sleep with?"

Kimi: "First?"

More laughter.

SHAD & BENJI'S APARTMENT

More beers are out along with a variety of sandwiches. There's now a very large roast beef sandwich, a meatball sandwich, and a tuna melt. Shad has got his laptop on the coffee table and they have Jackson on a video call. Jackson is in a spa tub in a spa-like bathroom.

Without food in front of him, Jackson can only consider the puzzle. "No doubt. I concur completely. The corned beef, coleslaw and Russian dressing at 2nd Ave Deli. For sure. But have you guys ever had a proper Arabic Sandwich on Arabic bread with spiced lamb and a yogurt mint sauce?"

Benji:" No."

Jackson: "So good. I love lamb. Oh... a great gyro. Don't you just crave that sometimes?"

Shad: "I got one. This is good. OK. Anyone ever go to a low country boil?"

Jackson: I'm not familiar with this."

Shad, now deep in delicious thought, explains, "There's a big boiling pot filled with crawfish, spicy sausage, potatoes, corn, asparagus, garlic, boil spices. It all gets dumped onto a long table covered in newspaper. You grab a piece of crusty French bread, smear the garlic on it like butter, then shove in a piece of sausage, some crawfish, maybe a piece of asparagus. Holy shit, it's good!"

They all consider the flavors Shad just described. It's like going into a food coma without actually eating the food.

Then, from deep in his own world, Benji says, "But which of the girls would you sleep with?

Jackson: "I see you're still hungry."

AFTERMATH

THE JOY'S APARTMENT

The Joy and Kimi are laying on the sofa. They're asleep on each other, in a state of disarray from the night before. Kimi's mask is hanging off one ear. The sound of people in line for the market is wafting into the room. The Joy slowly comes to life and looks around. She thinks, "What the hell happened last night? Oh, yeah. That was fun." Kimi is out cold. The Joy whispers in her sleeping ear, "I knew you'd pick me."

JACKSON'S APARTMENT

Jackson, with some form of smoothie in hand and dressed in Adidas workout pants, no shirt and cycling shoes, shuffles zombie-like to his Peloton bike. His cycling shoes make a clicking sound as he goes. He puts his smoothie in the cupholder and starts pedaling slowly. A message comes up on the screen. He has a challenge from Steph to beat her time from earlier this morning. He smiles to himself.

SHAD & BENJI'S APARTMENT

Benji is back on the sofa, wearing what he had on the previous night. Nothing has been cleaned up. He's holding his bowl of sourdough starter and watching the news. As his stress level escalates he starts rocking with the bowl. To no one, he starts repeating, "It's all going wrong. It's all going wrong."

Finally, he changes to another news channel. No help there. One more try. It's all bad news. "It's all going wrong. It's all going wrong." Make it stop. He turns off the TV and pulls out his phone. He finds anime *Food Wars* on his phone. It's like regular anime but with more of an *Iron Chef-*like cooking battle. This is helpful. He can handle this.

KIMI'S CORNER

Kimi is one with the La-Z-Boy. She's working on a computer sketch for a floral mask. When she finishes the design, she adds it to three others from her product line. Four masks. That's a good number to start with. She can do them in black and white and in color. So that's eight options. The black and white ones will cost her less in printing but she figures she can charge the same because they look equally cool. Maybe cooler. While she's in mid- entrepreneurial thought, she hears The Joy moving around the kitchen making her regular irregular breakfast concoction. Kimi thinks, "Please don't talk to me. Please don't talk to me."

No such luck. She can hear The Joy walking over to the curtain. "Hey, girlfriend."

Kimi calls out, "I'm busy."

The Joy calls back, "But don't you want to talk?"

Kimi does not. "Nope."

"I made you breakfast."

"Not hungry." Kimi sits waiting to see if The Joy will just go away, even though she knows better.

"I really think we need to talk."

"We don't."

"Then this will just be hanging out there."

"OK."

"OK, we can talk?"

"Nope."

"You know, I don't appreciate being treated like your girlfriend."

"Then don't act like her."

End of conversation. The Joy walks away, then calls out from across the apartment, "I'm giving your breakfast to The Fred. He appreciates me." Then to the cat, "Don't you? We hate mean Aunt Kimi."

Kimi relaxes. Thank God that's over. She goes to her print-on-demand site and starts to upload her mask designs. Figuring out the platform is confusing but she struggles her way through. For her online store, she has to write a short paragraph for each design, add pricing and key words. What a pain in the ass. None of it is straightforward and just when she thinks she's done, there is a new hoop to jump through. She's sure that dumber people than her have figured this out. She thinks, "I'm a fucking idiot." She has to stop herself several times from throwing her computer against the wall. She knows it would solve nothing, but the potential for immediate satisfaction holds a certain appeal. She likes throwing. No. Press on. Then...

The Joy flings the privacy curtain open and blurts, "Lady, we need to talk. If we don't talk this thing will just be hanging out there like a...a thing that's hanging there."

Kimi, annoyed that she's not done with this. "Oh, Christ."

"Aren't you Catholic?

"Hmm?"

"Well, I didn't think that your people took the Lord's name in vain."

"Well, you're Episcopalian. I didn't think your people...I actually don't know what your people do." Kimi tries to be calming. "I think the smart thing is to just let this go."

"That's not healthy."

"Fuck health. I say, ignoring shit is healthy."

"So it didn't mean anything to you?

Kimi shakes her head and explains, "The point is, it didn't mean anything to you. You were drunk and exploring. For you, last night was just a joy, right? Correction, a *The* Joy ride. Fine. It's been on your mind. You scratched the itch. You know what I did last night? Any guesses?"

The Joy is silent.

Kimi blurts, "I cheated on my girlfriend. Wear that one around the house!"

They both stare at each other. Yeah.

STEPH'S APARTMENT

Steph is at her computer with her oversized handbag at her feet. She's now got two TV screens in her dining area and they're both on with the sound off. One screen is on Bloomberg and the other is on *Call The Midwife*. She's looking up information for a news story on the economics of restaurants and if they'll be able to survive. How many New York City restaurants have closed so far?

She gets a text and checks her phone. It's from her mother. It reads, "Dear Stephanie, your aunt tracked the challah and it's in Camden. You should get it tomorrow. Don't forget to say thank you. It's a big deal. Love, your mother. P.S. my friend Terri Maglionni showed me how to text. She's Italian...but very nice." Steph just shakes her head.

Then, another text. It's her mother again. It reads, "Dear Stephanie, I didn't want to disturb you at work so I texted. Love, your mother." Wow. Steph will not be thanking that nice Italian lady.

But wait. There's more. Here comes another text. Steph's concerned that her mother's new texting skills are going to get way out of hand, but sees it is from a co-worker. It reads, "The shit is about to hit the fan. Duck!" Steph would rather have heard from her mother again.

SHAD & BENJI'S APARTMENT/BATHROOM

Shad is in the bathroom on the can. He's eating the remnants of a sandwich from the previous night and watching a financial scroll on his iPad. The numbers mean something to him, but not to most people. He stares at the screen, eats and thinks. His cell rings. He's now balancing the iPad on his lap and holding the sandwich and his cell. It's Christopher, from the office.

Shad answers, "Big C. What's up?"

Christopher sounds way less stressed than he does on a work call. "Oh, you know. Not watching baseball. Not watching golf."

"I think golf is talking about coming back."

"That would be cool. Listen, I have a question for you, but it's gotta be between you and me."

"Shoot."

Not convinced, Christopher asks, "So you'll keep this between you and me?"

"I don't even know what this is, yet. But, yeah. You and me."

Christopher spills, "I'm thinking about leaving the team."

Shad's taken aback, "Dude, seriously? Damn."

"I'm thinking of getting out of New York. Be bigger fish in a smaller pond. What do you think? I really trust your opinion."

"Give me a second to process...I love it. Where you thinking?"

"I have a lead in South Carolina. And here's the thing, they're looking for people and I told them about you."

Shad lets this sink in. Is this the change he was looking for? It's a huge step. His friends and family are here. But man...He might actually matter in someplace new. "I gotta think about this." As Shad thinks, his iPad slips off his lap and clanks onto the bathroom tile.

"Dude, are you on the can?"

Trying to maintain his cover, Shad says, "What? No."

Christopher is matter-of-factly, "It's all good. I am too."

STEPH'S APARTMENT

Steph hasn't moved. Her phone is still in her hand and she's staring at the doom-filled text. She runs through all of her actions in her head. Did she do anything wrong? Say, something she shouldn't have? Put something in an email and shared it with the wrong person? Oh, my God, this is brutal. Finally, she starts going through her emails. But not finding something has no "Aha!" moment to it and is not an end. And she finds nothing.

Should she call Janis? No. Wait. Maybe it'll be just something small. Maybe it will just blow over. She knows it won't, but is not interested in hurrying the bad news. She turns up the volume on *Call The Midwife* and tries to get sucked into the drama of others. It starts to work. She feels the civility of the writing relaxing her. Then, there's a scene in a bathroom and a clear, horrifying thought hits Steph. "It's the toilet paper. She knows I've been stealing toilet paper. Shit!"

THE JOY'S APARTMENT/BEDROOM

The Joy's bedroom is half hair salon, half sleeping lounge. A stylist's chair is positioned in front of a large standing mirror and to the side is a bed and large armoire. Most things are draped in thin, colorful scarves. The Joy currently has Dennis, a very large, tattooed biker-guy in her styling chair. Dennis wears lots of leather and metal. Not a guy you want to come across in a dark alley...or in your styling chair. But, The Joy has a familiarity and ease with him. She's giving him a scalp massage and he is relatively blissed-out. She asks, "Does it make me a homewrecker?"

Dennis thinks before responding, "Not really. They never lived together, so there's no home, ergo, you can't be a homewrecker. That's simple math."

The Joy considers this. "I can work with that...Thanks Dennis."

"Any time. You just keep doin 'what you're doin'."

JACKSON'S APARTMENT

It's night. Jackson is on his large balcony holding out his phone. It's angled so his parents, on the other end of the line, can see how empty the streets are in Manhattan.

Jackson says, "See, Mommy. Empty. It's completely bizzare."

Jackson's parents are physically stunning people. No surprise there. They look healthy and wealthy. They're standing on the balcony of their flat in the UAE. For them, it's morning.

Mr. Asghar sounds taken with what he sees. "Oh, my. Mother...look at that. I never thought I'd see Park Avenue empty. It's the same here, son. Wait, I'll show you." Mr. Asghar turns his phone and shows Jackson how no one is on the street there, either. "How about that? They closed the airport to passengers, you know? Only cargo in and out."

"I heard that."

Mrs. Asghar chimes in with a mother's concern, "You don't look good, Jacky. Are you eating?"

"Of course, Mommy. I can order whatever I want and Jeffery usually brings it up personally. I'm fine. I'm just bored."

Mr. Asghar offers, "Now would be a good time for you to take up your studies again. You've had your fun. You could use this time wisely."

"Father..."

Mrs. Asghar turns to her husband. "Leave him alone. Can't you see that he has a lot of stress right now." She looks back at her son." Being in that big apartment all by yourself, we should have your sister Ruby come up and stay with you."

"No, Mommy, I don't need Ruby. I'm fine."

Mrs. Asghar reasons, "She could cook for you. She needs purpose. Your other sisters are all married and Ruby is..."

Mr. Asghar cuts in, "She's like a drug on the market. That's what she is. You'd be doing us a favor, son. We're very worried about her."

Jackson suggests, "Perhaps Ruby likes being single?"

That makes no sense to Mrs. Asghar. "What nice girl likes being single?"

STEPH'S APARTMENT

Steph is getting on her Peloton. She's dressed in her best workout gear and has a towel, sports water bottle with her station logo on it, and her earbuds. When her screen comes on she sees that there's a message from Jackson. He beat her challenge and has a new one for her. She fantasizes about Jackson's form for a moment. That's a nice thought. OK, let's see if I can do this.

Her cell rings and she sees that it's Janis. She thinks, "Not right now. This is my time. I'll put off the bad news just a bit longer."

SHAD & BENJI'S APARTMENT

Shad emerges from his bedroom in a technical T-shirt and shorts. He's just given himself what he's calling his jail-cell workout: a run, some pushups and bit of ab work. He sees Benji just standing at the fridge with the door open. He watches Benji for a while to see if he'll do anything. Nope.

Shad calls out, "Dude, you window shopping or are you looking for something specific?"

"What do you care?"

"We share an electric bill. You're running it up holding the door open. Close the door until you know what you want."

"You sound like my mother."

"You smell like a boy's camp cabin. Bro, why don't you change the shirt? You're getting ripe."

"You're not the boss of me."

Shad goes to the fridge, shoots Benji a look, and closes the door. Like a teacher, Shad says, "Watch how it's done." He places his finger on his chin and says thoughtfully, "I think I'd like something to drink. But what? I know, a beer. I think I'd like a beer. Now that I know what I'm looking for, I think I'll open the refrigerator." Shad opens the fridge and looks at the top shelf where the beer usually lives. Nothing. "Mother...Are we out of beer?"

Benji shrugs. "I think so."

Shad stares at his roommate and thinks that it might not be so hard to move away after all.

SON OF ZOOM

THE JOY'S APARTMENT

As The Joy, now with jet black hair, prepares her video cocktail, she keeps looking over to Kimi's closed curtain. Not having a conversation to clear the air is killing her. Was it her fault? Should she apologize? Should she make Kimi a drink? Why can't Kimi just say what's on her mind so they can move on? This isn't fun at all. Life's too short for this.

She finishes setting up the laptop and puts a cocktail on either side. No way Kimi will be too upset to accept a cocktail mixed in the spirit of friendship. The Joy gets in position on her bar stool and enters the video call. No one. She looks over to Kimi's curtain. Nothing.

Finally, Steph's screen comes on. But no sound. She fiddles for a moment, "How about now?"

The Joy is relieved to see her. "I was beginning to wonder where all my friends went."

Steph asks, "Where's Kimi?"

"Oh, she'll be here."

Steph thinks back." The other night was so much fun. I didn't know how much I needed that. Paid for it the next day, though."

For different reasons, The Joy says, "Yeah, me too."

Steph looks at her phone. Janis is texting her. Shit. She ignores it and pockets her phone.

Shad's screen comes on. He's in his bedroom. He also fumbles with the settings until he can be heard. "Hey, gang."

The Joy: "Hey yourself, Wolf of Wall Street."

Steph: "No Benji?"

Shad: "We're on separate screens this time around."

Steph: "Trouble in paradise...or has he just not changed his shirt yet?"

Jackson's screen comes on. Jackson has on a cape and a T-shirt with a question mark. He salutes the group. "Greetings from the Enigma Ninja."

The Joy is delighted and claps. "You look fantastic."

Shad: "I feel this requires an explanation."

Steph: "Agreed."

Jackson: "Not just yet. I want to wait until we're all on."

Benji's screen comes on. He's in his loft bedroom. The lights are off except for his desk lamp, which is on the floor pointing up, bathing him in drama. His thick, dark hair is arranged over one eye so he resembles one of the characters from his anime shows. His speech is somewhat altered as well. It's clipped and sinister. "Good evening."

The Joy: "Did we agree to dress up? I love dress up."

Steph: "I heard nothing."

Benji: "Am I last to arrive?"

Mockingly, Shad says, "No, strange one. We await Kimi."

Benji: "You mock me?"

Shad: "You bet."

There's silence as they all wait for Kimi. Everyone is looking at everyone else as if they're about to be introduced for the first time. Finally, The Joy calls out in her most pleasant voice, "Kimi, we're all here. We're waiting for you to get started." More waiting. More silence. "Kimi girl?"

Sensing an opportunity, Steph starts in. "Well, if no one is going to say anything, Janis is on the war path. First, she insists that if we don't come into the office, we're not committed to the job. Then she refuses to come to the office because she's too important to expose herself to germs. Seriously? Then we're all home because some of the people who went in got sick. Now, she's mad at me for God knows what. I think I might lose my job. Then where will I be?"

Shad: "Exactly where you are right now. In the apartment your daddy got you."

Steph: "Oh shit, I forgot my wine. I knew this felt extra hard." Steph heads to her kitchen in the back of the frame and grabs an open wine bottle and a glass. When she returns, she addresses Shad. "And seriously Shad? For your information, I pay my way...a good part of my way."

More silence. The Joy calls out again, "Kimi Girl, are you joining us? People are in costume."

Kimi finally emerges from her corner. The Joy was expecting her to look like she's mad, but she seems the same as always. Not great. Just the same. Kimi takes her place next to The Joy and sips her cocktail. "Sorry I'm late, kids."

The Joy gives Kimi a quizzical look as if to ask, "Are we okay now and I just didn't know it?"

Steph: "What's up? You two need some space?"

At the same time Benji and Shad say, "Yes."

The Joy: "What's with you and the questions?"

Steph: "I'm in the news."

Jackson: "I have some news. I'm going to apply for *American Ninja Warrior*. I am the Enigma Ninja."

Kimi: "Of course, you are."

Benji: "Sadly, that moniker is taken."

Jackson: What?"

Benji: "There already exists an Enigma Ninja."

Bummed, Jackson shakes his head. "My bad. I didn't do my research. OK. How about the Park Avenue Ninja?"

Kimi: "I make no judgments."

Shad: "Sure you do."

Jackson: "I'm ignoring this negativity. I have set up an obstacle course in the apartment and I'm training every day. I just need a good sob story."

Kimi: "I got one."

Quietly to Kimi, The Joy say: "Do you really want to be airing your dirty laundry?"

Steph: "I think she does."

The Joy fears she's about to be outed for being a homewrecker without the home. Everyone is going to hate her. She couldn't take that. But, Kimi goes in a new direction. "No one wants my masks. I've failed again." The Joy releases a breath, relieved that the bad news isn't about her.

Jackson: "I don't understand. Am I missing information?"

Kimi: "I designed masks. With flowers. I put them up on Etsy but no one's buying. I really thought I had something. It combined two things I'm passionate about, flowers and not dying."

Steph feels for her friend. "Well, how long did you give it? How did you promote it?"

Shad: "Did you target a particular audience? Did you do A/B testing?"

Steph: "What social platforms are you using?"

Kimi: "I designed masks and put them on Etsy. That's it. I don't know anything about this other shit."

The Joy: "See, you're not a failure. You're just highly ignorant."

Kimi: "I'm so glad I joined you all tonight."

Jackson: "I don't think you mean that."

Benji: "I'll purchase a mask."

Kimi: "Alright. Alright. Enough about me. Benji, what the fuck with the up-lighting?"

Benji: "Do you like it?"

Kimi: "Yes?"

Shad: "He's becoming a living anime character."

Defensively Benji asks Shad: "Does it bother you?"

Shad: "Yes. It's annoying as hell."

Benji: "Annoying like when you bang on the wall and won't let a friend jack off?"

Kimi: "I may need popcorn for this."

Shad: "Well, you got me there. I confess. I banged on the wall to stop you from banging on yourself. Maybe if you weren't so damn huge and didn't make so much noise."

Steph: "Seriously, you know a sound that I hate?"

Shad: "The sound of you saying "seriously" every two seconds?"

Steph is stopped in her tracks, "What?"

The Joy: "You do use that word a lot."

Kimi: "And you do that tongue against your back teeth sound every time you're about to say something condescending."

The Joy, without realizing it, makes the exact sound Kimi is talking about before she says, "Is that what you really want to talk to me about? Or is there something you need to say to clear the air?"

Kimi: "No. That's what I wanted to say."

Steph: "Are you sure you don't want to clear the air? We're happy to listen."

Jackson: "Wait, I have one. I hate when every commercial talks about 'These undertain times." What times are certain? Nothing in this life is guaranteed. It makes no sense.

Steph: "She was about to clear the air."

Kimi: "I wasn't."

Steph: "Fine. What's everyone watching? I need distractions."

The Joy: "I love *The Crown*. Everyone is just so...royal."

Steph: "I've heard that's good. I'm bingeing on *Call The Midwife*, but I think I'll be through every season in days. I've seen so many episodes and so many births, I think I could deliver myself a baby now if I had to. Serious."

Shad: "Seriously?"

Steph: "No one likes you, Shad."

Benji: "I've been watching *The Great British Baking Show*."

Shad: "But that's not in space...or animated."

Jackson: "Let's not speak ill of sci-fi."

Benji: "Speak ill if you must. It's a lovely show and I'm learning a lot. How is everyone's sourdough? Little Douglas is growing bigger every day."

Shad: "And I want my dog back."

Benji: "No backsies."

Shad: "Oh, there's gonna be backsies."

Steph: "Do you two need a moment?"

Shad: "I think it's time for more than a moment. I gotta go." Shad's screen goes black.

The Joy: "This is so sad. I hate arguments."

Benji: "I think I'm going to depart as well. Bye guys." Benji's screen goes black.

Kimi: "I'm ready to call it, too." Kimi raises her glass, gets up, gets a pint of ice cream from the fridge and disappears into her corner.

The Joy: "No. This is supposed to be our happy, together time. *Ach.* Well, next week I demand that everyone be happy. Got it? Maybe I'll wear a costume." The Joy's screen goes black.

After a moment, Steph says: "Well, Mr. Park Avenue Ninja, looks like it's just you and me."

Jackson is suddenly looking extra sexy and emboldened.

THE WTF DAYS

THE JOY'S APARTMENT

The Joy and Kimi are going through their life routines in the same space, but separately. The Joy is in the kitchen creating some sort of meal. Per The Joy style, food items are going in a bowl that don't typically spend time together. Kimi sees this while going for her plain granola. She's no longer fazed by The Joy's bizarre food concoctions and has no need to comment. She takes her granola over to her corner and is gone. The Joy looks over for a moment then heads to the sofa.

She hears something. What is that noise? The Joy gets up and tries to locate the source of a persistent squeak. She's getting warmer... Warmer... The Joy finally tracks the sound to the box fan that's below the window by the fire escape. She turns it off and turns it on again. No better. Should she hit it? Sure. Why not? She hits it several times, but with no change. Then a solution comes to her. The Joy heads to the kitchen, goes into an upper cabinet and returns to the window with a bottle of cooking oil. She lets the fan run, pours some of the oil in and waits. Hey. That did the trick. Brilliant!

The Joy returns to the sofa, pleased with her craftiness. And then...the fan stops dead. Damn it.

SHAD & BENJI'S APARTMENT

Silence reigns. Benji is in the kitchen stirring a soup and Shad is coming out of his bedroom. Both have their heads down, each staring at their own device. As Shad heads for the kitchen, Benji stops his work and heads for the bathroom. When they pass each other behind the sofa, the roommates each keep their focus 100% locked on their own device. It's chilly in here.

THE JOY'S APARTMENT/FIRE ESCAPE

Kimi has her laptop and phone with her on the fire escape. There's no clarinet music at the moment. She's trying to figure out how to market her flower masks online. The first articles she reads are about how easy online ads are. Articles like, "10 Simple Steps To Crushing It With Online Advertising," and "What Everyone Needs To Know To Kill It In Digital Marketing," and "How To Stand Out From All The Online Noise." She then reads opposing articles with titles like, "Why Facebook Ads Are Useless," and "The Layperson Can'T Hit The Moving Target Of Online Ads," and "You'll Never Stand Out In All The Noise." Could she feel more disheartened?

Her cell rings. It's Milli's tone. *We Are Family* by the Pointer Sisters from back in the 19-whatevers. But it's their song. Kimi picks up, happy for the distraction. "What!"

Sounding down, Milli says, "Hey you."

"What's up?"

"I just needed to hear a happy voice."

"And you picked me? That's just sad."

Milli laughs at that then turns serious, "No, really. Things at the hospital are so damn bleak. People are dying. We're running out of essential supplies. We're running out of beds. We're asking sick people to stay home. I've never felt so helpless. Or useless. Let me be clear. This is not like the flu."

Kimi takes it in, "I'm sorry. I wish I could help."

"You listening. That helps. I'm trying to not keep dumping on Shey. And I can't talk around the kids. It's just all so frustrating...Tell me something happy."

Kimi tries to think of something that will sound playful to share with her sister, but comes up empty.

"Tell me about your life as a mask mogul?"

"I thought you wanted to talk about something happy...Masks. I really thought I had something. But the maze of trying to decipher how to sell my designs...It's an entirely other skill that I clearly do not possess. I'm banging my head."

"Sorry. I'll change the subject. How's Carmen?"

"And, you're two for two."

Sounding dejected, Milli says, "You're not cheering me up."

"Well, back at ya."

The sisters sit on the phone in silence. They know that each has nothing to help the other. But being together, even at a distance, makes them feel less like they're drowning alone. At least they have someone who cares to witness it. Maybe it will be okay. Maybe.

STEPH'S APARTMENT

Steph is mindlessly staring into her refrigerator. She's wearing what has become her new at-home uniform: black yoga pants and a loose-fitting, workout tank top. Her phone rings. What now?

"Yeah, mom."

A male voice responds, "It can't be your father?"

Surprised, Steph says, "Dad, hey. Sure. What's up?"

"Your mother's very upset."

"Why? What's wrong?"

Mur asks, "Did you get your aunt's challah?"

Cautiously, Steph answers, "Yes?"

"Well, you didn't tell your mother you got it. It would be nice if you would call her and tell her that it got there OK, so she can stop asking me every five minutes when I think you're going to call or if I think something went wrong."

"OK. I'll call her."

"Thank you. Because if I have to hear one more time about your aunt's goddamn challah…"

"I'll call her right now."

With that, Murray's tone relaxes. "That would be good. Thank you. I love you.

Goodbye." Murray hangs up. Steph looks at her phone, shakes her head and thinks, "Seriously?"

SHAD & BENJI'S APARTMENT/SHAD'S BEDROOM

While Shad's on a call with his brother, Chad, he paces his bedroom. As when he paced before, it's a bit of an attempt to find something that will help him keep his sanity. But this time he's not aware that he's doing it. He's starting to feel like a prisoner in his own apartment. He says, "I'm starting to feel like a prisoner in my own apartment."

Chad asks, "Is that really why you called me? When was the last time I heard from you?"

Shad stops pacing. "I don't know. When was the last time I heard from you?"

Chad was ready for that. "February 9th, 2 p.m. I invited you to come down for BBQ. Remember? But that was too pedestrian for you. You were way too busy with your life in the big city."

"I never said that."

"No. What you said was," Chad does his best Shad impersonation, "Oh...Chad, that sounds great, yeah, but I have a big thing early tomorrow. You get it, bro."

Shad feels caught in the act. "That's quite a memory."

"Yep. A boring, suburban accountant's memory. So what do you want?"

"You're so cold. What I want...what I was looking for is your advice. Your boring suburban advice on moving out of the city into the boring suburbs."

Chad's surprised. "Really?"

"Yeah. I may have an opportunity and I wanted your take on...well...are you happy?"

"Wow. We're going deep now." Chad's done being offended and gives the question real thought. "Yeah. I guess I'm happy. I love my wife. I have three great kids that are way more entertaining than anything on TV. I'm near the folks. I like my job."

"You *like* your job?"

"Yeah. I *like* my job. I'm not you. I was never looking to set the world on fire. I have no big adrenaline rush needs. Maybe that's why Dad connects with Joe the most, with coaching football on top of being firstborn and all. Me? I like being an accountant. It's a nice firm. The benefits are good. I *love* my family. I *like* my job."

"I don't have a family."

"Guess I didn't help."

Japanese music is coming through the wall. There's also some stomping. Shad can only imagine that Benji is working on his TikTok moves again. Good God." No. I think, you did help."

"OK, well, don't be such a stranger."

"No, man. I won't. Thanks." They hang up. Shad has a lot to think about. The music and the banging doesn't help. Or maybe it does.

SHAD & BENJI'S APARTMENT

Yep. Benji's doing a TikTok dance.

JACKSON'S APARTMENT/BEDROOM

Damn, that's a decadent bed. All the extra-thick, fluffy bedding is in varying shades of cream and gold. The entire room is grand. Jackson has taken over his parents' bedroom. Why not? No one was using it. He's laying spreadeagle, trying to take up as much of the bed as possible. Impossible. The thing is huge. Daylight is streaming in the room but he doesn't feel like he's in a hurry to make anything happen. He feels the ripples of his abs. They're there, but is he losing tone. He's going to have to work on that...but later.

He reaches for his cell and surfs around for a bit. A post on Instagram takes him to a video on YouTube which takes him to five more videos on YouTube. Enough of that. Let's hear from the masses. Without moving his torso, he reaches for the TV remote which is in the covers and hits power. A news woman, sitting alone at a desk in a home office, is talking about how an extra $600 will be made available in unemployment benefits to New Yorkers. This does not affect his world. Click. A newsperson, this time a man, is sitting at a studio desk where another newsperson is standing at least six feet away. He says that Mayor Cuomo signed an executive order requiring all New York State residents must wear face masks in public places where social distancing is not possible. Will that affect his world? He hasn't left his apartment in weeks. Distancing hasn't been the challenge.

As the newsperson goes on, Jackson can feel something balled up under his right shoulder. He reaches back and pulls out a robin's egg blue, lace bra. He holds it up and smiles remembering how it got there. That was fun. He thinks, "OK, maybe I haven't been completely great at being on top of distancing. But I was completely great at being on top." He smiles at his own joke. No one ever tells him that he's funny, but he thinks he is.

THE JOY'S APARTMENT

The Joy is on her sofa wearing a flowy getup that looks rather Middle Eastern. She finds that when things are bothering her, it can help elevate the mood if she gets more colorful in her wardrobe. So far, it's not working. Too much time to think. Too few places to go. She hears sounds from outside and goes to the window. It's the market people. She listens for a while at their inane, redundant conversations. Then, she excitedly dashes over to Kimi's curtained-off corner and calls in, "Hey, there are some really annoying people in the market line today. Wanna come harass the Lulu Ladies with me?"

From behind the curtain, Kimi calls, "I'm good...Do I smell popcorn?"

The Joy looks over to the now dead fan that's full of cooking oil. Innocently she calls back, "No. But...want me to make some?"

"I'm good."

Deflated, The Joy returns to the sofa. She looks through her appointments and sees that she has nothing for the rest of the day. Out loud, she says, "I'm so bored." Without getting up she looks around the room. Guess she'll have to order something to be overnighted.

SHAD & BENJI'S APARTMENT

Shad's perched halfway up Benji's loft ladder. He knocks on the wall and waits. He knocks louder. Nothing. He finally climbs the rest of the way up and finds Benji lying on his bed, wearing headphones with J-pop seeping out.

Shad looks into the loft space. "Sorry to interrupt. Got a second?"

Benji takes his headphones off slowly. "Hey. I was wearing headphones to not bug you."

"That's cool. I just have to talk to you about something."

Like he's talking to his parents, Benji asks, "I'm in trouble?"

"No. No. But I need to talk to you."

"Come on in. Oh, wait." Benji gets up and scoops the massive pile of stuff from his bed and dumps it onto the floor so Shad will have a place to sit down. "Mi casa..."

Shad wonders if Benji has been sleeping next to all of that stuff. Probably. How's he going to put this? No good way. He opts for blurting. "I'm thinking of leaving New York." Wow, that seemed abrupt to both of them. It's like the bad news is now a third roommate that no one likes. The announcement is followed by a lot of looking at the floor.

Benji offers, "You can have your dog back."

"It's not about the dog."

"Then, can I keep him?"

"No." Shad tries to regroup his thinking." It's not about the dog, or you. It's me."

"I've heard that line seven, no, eight times before."

"I'm not happy," Shad admits. "Maybe it's the pandemic making me crazy. Or maybe it's just making me see things that are wrong with my life that I couldn't see before. I'm just repeating myself. And I'm not taken seriously. My boss doesn't respect me. I'm not going to meet anyone during lockdown. I just didn't want to blindside you. I wanted you to know that I'm considering it so you can make a plan."

"What kind of plan?"

" Well, if I do move, you're gonna need a new roommate. Or you'll have to move in with someone else."

"No one else likes me."

Shad's struck by how matter-of-factly Benji just said that. "Dude, that's not true. We all like you."

"But it took a really long time. You didn't like me in school. We just moved in because we remembered each other from home and I could afford the rent."

This is getting sadder by the second. "We just traveled in different circles." Shad gets up to leave. "And I may not move, but I might...and you'll need to have a plan." He leaves Benji alone in his room.

STEPH'S APARTMENT

Steph is on a video call with coworkers. She's angled her computer so her background is a corner with one of the walls being her window wall. In front of the other wall is her side board which has a few strategically placed awards on it and a plant. On the wall above it, she's moved her framed poster of a Lichtenstein depiction of Wonder Women. In it, Wonder Woman has a tear in her eye and a talk bubble that reads, "OH, CLARK! WHY CAN'T WE JUST GET MARRIED AND MAKE SUPER BABIES?" It used to hang in Steph's bedroom.

Most of the people on the call seem to have dialed in their video call backgrounds. Corners are popular. Bookends sandwich carefully selected books. Janis is still looking like a hot mess. So is her background. There seem to be blankets and pillows everywhere. Steph thinks, man, she's letting herself go. Janis's weight is up, her complexion is off. And can she not find her hair brush?

Janis continues, "That's right. Governor Cuomo just extended the stay-at-home order through May 15th. May 15th is our new official end date. But, we all know, this thing isn't close to having an end date. Now, Bill's team is dropping like flies. That's what they get for having to be in the office. They sure showed us what dedication looks like. You all can thank me later for letting you work from home. But that means that some of us are going to have to cover for some of them. I sent a revised punch list to everyone one. You all got it, right?"

Everyone voices their own form of a yes answer.

Janis asks, "Anyone have any questions?'

After a pause, Steph chimes in, "I don't see that I have any field reports scheduled."

Janis stifles Steph, "Was that a question?"

The other participants on the call are trying to look away, as if that will provide some privacy for the two. Teddy, an older fellow on the team absently picks his nose on screen. It doesn't go unnoticed, but no one calls him out on it.

Steph tries again. "I just think it's strange that we're doing our assignments and covering for Bill's team and I don't have any field reports."

Squashing Steph's second attempt, Janis shakes her head. "Still not in the form of a question...OK, team, since we have no *questions* and a shitload to cover, I'm calling this. Oh, Ray, I need you to get back to me ASAP with the info from Mr. Bloomberg's ten-and-a-half-mill education contribution." Passing her hand downwards in front of her face, Janis declares, "And...scene!" Janis's screen goes black. Everyone looks around. A few, "See ya's" are said and they all exit the call.

Steph sits for a moment trying to figure out what her next move is. She's stumped. Then she gets a text. It's Janis." Can you talk now or are you ducking this call, too?"

Steph texts back, "Not ducking." She waits an uncomfortable ten minutes in her chair before Janis calls.

Steph grabs it." What's up?"

Janis answers smugly. "See, I knew you knew how to ask a question."

Fearing the answer, Steph decides to pretend she knows nothing about the toilet paper. They can't prove anything. Admit nothing. Better than that, be aggressive. When in doubt, re-raise. With her strategy decided, Steph charges forward. "What's going on? What horrible thing did I do?"

"Don't you want to guess?"

"I check my emails, my texts, I couldn't find anything that I'd have to apologize for. So just tell me what I said and I'll apologize for it."

After a long, uncomfortable moment, Janis reveals the issue. "I don't appreciate you sharing my private life with the entire office. When I tell you something, it's in the strictest confidence."

Steph is baffled by this. She was waiting for Janis to go on a rant about stealing from the company. And if not that, maybe she would say something that would trigger some horrible revelation of something Steph did, but had forgotten. Something truly unforgivable. She'd done the "Ida spiral" down that rabbit hole the other night. The one where one awful thing leads to another awful thing and creates a domino effect of tragic events ending with someone laying at the bottom of a stairwell with their head cracked open...which was how all of Ida's worst-case-scenario musings ended. But, what the hell was this? Private life?

Janis gets impatient. She's almost yelling. "Well? Do you have anything to say?"

"No. I mean, I would never say anything to anyone about your private life."

"And I'm just supposed to take you at your word? Put me on video. I hate yelling at you and not seeing your face."

Steph switches to video call. "Here. This is my face telling you that I'm not the one who shared your information."

And now Janis is yelling. "Then can you tell me how Barry in editing knows about my fight with Margaret? Or Davis the camera guy, or Trudy? Fucking Trudy! Do you know how this is going to fuck me? They're calling it Tapioca-Gate. No one's going to take me seriously. I'm going to lose my credibility and I blame you. *J'accuse!*"

Before Steph can respond, a young girl bounds through the frame behind Janis, singing loudly. Janis turns to the child with zero patience. "Hey, Sophie, I'm on a call. Zip it." Sophie disappears.

Surprised by the child, Steph ask, "Who's that?"

Janis rolls her eyes. "Margaret's kid."

Putting the pieces together Steph poses, "Was she quarantined in your guest bedroom with Margaret for two weeks?"

"What, you want to call child services, now?"

KIMI'S CORNER

Kimi's trying something new. She's working while sitting on her cube fridge with her feet up on the La-Z-Boy. Perhaps a new angle will help things. She's rewriting headlines for mask ads. She types, "Put a flower on your face...No one will think you're lying when you're wearing lilacs...Distract them with daisies...Cover your two lips with tulips...Buy my fucking masks you fuckheads!" OK, maybe that last one won't seal the deal.

Her phone vibrates. It's Carmen texting. "Hey [poop emoji] head!"

Kimi thinks she'd better respond to this. She's been avoiding Carmen. She's been avoiding everyone, really. Damn it. She texts back, "Nice likeness."

"Was wondering if you were ever going to talk to me. Where've you been?"

"Here."

"Don't make me pull it out of you. Talk to me."

"What do you want me to say?"

"How about anything?"

Kimi just stares at her phone for a while. She feels trapped. She'd rather focus on getting her business off the ground. Then she might feel like she has some control of her life again. But aren't relationships supposed to be important? Like, more important than work? That's what everyone says. But, commitment...She hates feeling backed against a wall. She's already stuck in a corner. Suddenly her corner seems like a metaphor for her entire life.

Kimi texts, "I slept with The Joy."

"Fuck you!"

SHAD & BENJI'S APARTMENT

Benji is leaning on the kitchen counter, cell phone in hand. Fluffers/Douglas is staring at him hoping for food or a little attention. He gets neither. Benji dials a number and anxiously waits for it to be picked up. He practices smiling while he waits. Finally, Patrick answers, "Benji?"

"Hey, Patrick."

Sounding like there's no reason for Benji to be calling, Patrick asks, "What's up, man?"

"I heard you might be looking for a roommate."

Patrick's slow to respond. "Ah, yeah. Well, Pete's moving to Colorado or some such shit. His bed's gonna be available in a couple of weeks. Then it'll just be the five of us. Well, Peggy might go back to her parents' place. She hasn't had work in like, forever. Fuckin 'restaurants, man." Over-explaining. The first sign of dodging an uncomfortable situation. Misdirection. The second sign.

Benji can only concur, "Yeah."

With little enthusiasm, Patrick asks, "Are you askin 'for you?"

"Yeah."

Trying to sound cool with Benji's ask, but not pulling it off, Patrick says, "I mean, like, I'd have to ask everyone if they're okay with you movin' in. You know. It would just be the right thing. I mean, I'd be cool with it. But, you know...roommates. Should be democratic and all."

This response is nothing new for Benji. What can he say? "Yeah. Sure."

"I mean, I don't have a problem with you...You can pay, right?"

"Yeah."

"Cool. Well, let me talk to everybody. May take a few days. Everybody's on a different schedule. But, yeah. Cool. Be well, man. Peace." Patrick hangs up.

Benji looks down at Fluffers/Douglas and just stares. Fluffers/Douglas stares back like he understands.

ANOTHER DAMN ZOOM CALL

THE JOY'S APARTMENT

Everyone is on the call. Everyone has a drink. No one is talking. Instead of being in the kitchen with The Joy, Kimi is on her computer in her corner. Shad is in his bedroom while Benji is in his loft. The only person on the call who looks good at all is Jackson. He has New York as his background. Steph still has her enviable level of attractiveness, but her stress is making her look less radiant and tired.

Shad finally breaks the silence, "So, May 15 now." He might as well have said, How 'bout those Mets.

Steph: "It's going to be longer than weeks...or months."

Shad: "What do you know?"

Steph: "Just prepare to sit tight for a while. We're not close to a vaccine, we're way behind on testing and people are now talking about how many years."

Kimi: "Mother of pearl!"

They all think about Steph's hard, cold tidbit. Then Steph adds, "Yep. You know whose business is starting to boom? Divorce lawyers."

Shad: "Make sense."

Benji: "I feel like you want a divorce?"

Shad: "Dude, it's not you."

Jackson: "Gentlemen, what's going on?"

Benji: "Shad's moving out."

Surprised, the gang all starts to over talk. Shad busts through the din. "No. Wait. I didn't say that. That's not...What I said was, I'm *considering* a job out of town and that you should *consider* what you will do if that were to happen."

The Joy: "You'd break up the band?"

Shad: "We're not a band."

The Joy: "But if we were, you'd be the one breaking it up."

Jackson: "Where's the job?"

Shad: "If I *were* to take it, it's in South Carolina."

Kimi: "And if you *weren't* to take it, where would it be then?"

With a bit of a knife thrust, Shad says, "Funny. How are mask sales going?"

Kimi: "I've made millions, thanks for asking."

Shad: "Sorry. That was wrong."

Kimi: "Wrong and sad and true. I can't sell a mask to save my soul."

The Joy: "That's where you're wrong. Drum roll." No one makes a sound. "Fine. I'll make my own drum roll." The Joy makes a sound that is nothing like a drum roll. Oh, well. From under the counter, she pulls out one of Kimi's flower masks and puts it on. "Tah-dah!"

Steph: "That's so sweet."

The Joy: "There. You no longer have to save your soul. I saved it."

Kimi is humbled. But it's not enough to pull her out of her depression. "Thank you. I appreciate the gesture."

Jackson: "I'll buy a mask."

Kimi: "Guys, I'm not looking for pity sales. Why don't we go back to talking about Shad abandoning us?"

Shad: "Thank you, Kimi."

Benji: "He's mad at me."

Shad: "Oh, my God! It's not about you. I'm trying to figure a few things out. I'm not growing here. I'm not doing anything important."

Benji: "What important thing are you going to do in the Palmetto state that you can't do here?"

Shad: "Well...I could be a big fish in a small pond."

On that note, everyone is silent again. Steph jumps in. "OK, I'll go. My boss thinks I'm sharing her private information with other people at work and she's blackballing me from the on-camera assignments."

The Joy: "Is she right? Are you?"

Steph: "You think I'm crazy? No, she's not right! I'm not an idiot. I know what would happen to my career if I played those games...Although it seems to be happening anyway."

Jackson: "Can I help?"

Kimi thinks, that's a strange question for Jackson to be asking. She considers confronting him, then thinks better of it. She's had enough of a spotlight on her for one call.

Steph: "No. But thanks. It's just so strange. I didn't even tell you guys the crazy shit she does for fear of it getting back to her."

The Joy: "What crazy shit does she do? You can tell us."

Kimi: "I would be totally up for hearing about someone else's crazy shit."

Shad: "I do think you should tell us."

Jackson: "Come on, guys. Don't push. It wouldn't be cricket."

Kimi: "OK, what's going on with you two?"

As innocently as possible Steph says, "What are you talking about?"

Kimi: "And there's my confirmation."

The Joy: "Am I missing something?"

Kimi: "Often."

Shad: "Wait. Are you two doing the deed?"

Steph: "Seriously. All of you. I don't have time for this. I have to go write a fake news story about a challah so my mother will stand down. I love you all...except Kimi. Bye." And with that, Steph's screen goes black.

Shad: "Just when it was getting good. Jackson?"

Jackson: "What?"

Shad: "Do you have anything to share with the class?"

Jackson: "Why, no. I don't." There's the sound of a woman singing in the background. Everyone hears it. They all look around uncomfortably. No one says anything but they're all thinking the same thing. Jackson had a fling with Steph and now has another girl in the apartment.

Shad: "Hey, that's fine. Your life is your business. Right?"

Jackson: "Thank you."

Sarcastically, Kimi says," This has certainly been a fun call. Do we want to keep doing these?"

Almost in a panic, The Joy jumps in, "Of course we do. It's a tradition."

Kimi: "A handful of weeks is not a tradition."

The Joy: "It so is."

Coming to The Joy's aid, Benji shares, "A tradition is a belief or a behavior passed down within a group...us, or society...not us, with symbolic meaning or special significance with origins in the past. How long in the past that behavior...in our case, has existed, is not relevant. Just that it existed. Therefore, our calls are, in fact, a tradition. And I would like to maintain that tradition."

The Joy: "Thank you, Benjamin, for that well thought-out argument. I concur."

Kimi: "Alrighty then. Until next time."

The Joy: "That's it?"

Jackson:" *Arrivederci*, all." Jackson raises his glass and signs off.

The Joy: "This part's always so sad."

The rest say goodbye and sign off.

LOOKING FOR SAVES

SHAD & BENJI'S APARTMENT

Benji comes in the front door with a package. He's wearing a different anime shirt, long shorts, a mask and bedroom slippers. Nothing matches. Not that he would know. He puts the package on the coffee table and opens it. It's his Wii from home. Score! "Thank, you, Mom!" Fluffers/Douglas gets excited for him. This is like gold. Benji scoops up the Wii and heads to Shad's room. But just before he calls in to show Shad, he thinks better of it. Shad probably won't want to play with him right now.

Benji takes the Wii back into the living room and sets it up. Maybe Shad will hear the unwrapping and come out to see what's going on. He'll have to be excited. But Shad doesn't come out. After it's all set up, Benji grabs his phone and texts Jackson. "Dude, my mom just sent me my Wii. Wanna play?"

Benji waits a long time, but Jackson doesn't respond. Finally, Benji picks up the Wii control and selects *Mario Karts,* number of players, one.

JACKSON'S APARTMENT/BEDROOM

Jackson is ascending the salmon ladder that he built in his bedroom. The ladder, as on *Ninja Warrior*, is like a ladder, but without rungs. To get up it, one has to hold a dowel in their hands and kip their body to jump the dowel to the next rung holders, one level up. Jackson's able to advance two levels before falling. Damn it. He sits on the floor and looks up. Let's try again. On his next attempt, he gets up three levels before falling. Shit. It looks so much easier on TV.

He decides to do a handstand against the wall opposite the ladder and stare at it. Perhaps the solution will come to him from his new pose. While upside down he can see under the bed. There are boxes. What did he put in those? He remembers. Old photos. He drops out of his hand stand and starts pulling out boxes. Most of these were put together by his mother and are like little filing drawers. Jackson randomly pulls out pictures. He sees their home in The United Arab Emirates. It's beautiful. He feels warm. He remembers his childhood being filled with love. There's a picture of his grandparents posing in their finery. They seem like they're from another world. Then a picture of his three sisters. The oldest one, Sarah, is holding a little baby boy. Him. He thinks about his family, and their families. Jackson then stares at the salmon ladder.

STEPH'S APARTMENT

Back on her Peloton bike, Steph is trying to solve the puzzle of who shared Janis's information. This is ridiculous. Is this what four years of college and interning and working long hours to prove herself and starting to get a little bit of traction has come to? It's so petty. Do we never grow up? Is it just high school over and over again? That's a depressing thought.

How far has she gone? Five miles. That's it? Did Jackson ride today? No intel. Fuck this. She gets off the bike and walks over to her computer. Standing there, she clicks onto her office mail. There's something from Bill. What now?

SHAD'S APARTMENT/SHAD'S BEDROOM

Shad is laying on his back on his bed, dressed for work. He's on his cell with Christopher.

Christopher's almost giddy. "I pulled the trigger."

Shad sits up. "What did Max say?"

"He was totally calm. He wished me well, said it was a good firm and that was it. I had this whole speech ready. I mean, I'd worked on it for days, but, nothing. It was so easy. I'm leaving in two weeks."

"Maybe you can shoot me that speech."

"Does that mean you're in?"

Without realizing it, Shad starts nodding. "I think so...You know, I wasn't sure until just now."

"Cool. Good luck, man. Call me after."

"Thanks, man. I will."

They hang up. Shad looks around his tiny room thinking, "I guess I'm really going to do this." He can hear Benji doing something in the living room. No. He can't worry about that. "Am I my brother's keeper?" OK. Maybe too dramatic.

Feeling almost emboldened, he gets up and goes to his computer. He shoots Max an email saying that he needs to schedule a talk. *Send*. Well, that's it. The deed is done. No backsies.

THE JOY'S APARTMENT

Kimi, with mask in place, is sitting on the window ledge listening in on the market line conversations. This is now one of the ways she clears her head. When she wants to just relax, it's the fire escape. When she needs a little stimulation, it's the front window. It's way better than TV. And there's Smoothie Guy. He seems as stressed as ever. It looks like he's jogging in place. There're the Tattoo Twins. Tough looking brother, so named by her for obvious reasons. They're arguing.

Twin #1 declares, "Almond milk is bullshit."

Twin #2 defends his position, "I can't tolerate lactose, and lactose-free milk is disgusting."

Twin #1 shares another point to his position. "Almond milk is disgusting."

Twin #2 retorts, "You're disgusting."

Guess that was too personal. Twin #1 drops his head. "Are you trying to be hurtful, because you are."

And, that's all it takes. Twin #2 says, "I'm sorry. But my cereal is really important to me." Twin #1 knows this to be true. The brothers stand quietly. End of argument.

Kimi thinks that was just a little bit of gold. She lets her mind drift and she starts thinking about Carmen. "Why am I such a Jerk? Or am I just a weenie and it's manifesting itself in jerk-like behavior? Still makes me a jerk." She's not happy with herself. She wants to call Carmen and try to explain herself, but how can she when she doesn't totally understand herself? And what if she pours her heart out and Carmen accepts her apology? She'll for sure want to move to the next level and that is just...fuck. Would it be so bad? It might. And then she'd have to get out of it and that would suck so much more. Carmen is so good, and funny, and sure. Why is she so fucking sure? Ahhh!

Kimi shakes her head and tries to focus on her market line people again. There's an older Chinese woman in line. She's been there at least once a week. The old woman waves at Kimi. Kimi waves back. Nothing big, but a wave. The woman smiles. The familiarity feels nice. This level of engagement is good. But then, right in the middle of starting to feel better, she spots the Lemon Ladies talking and pointing at her. They're clearly not saying anything nice.

Kimi calls to them, "You have something to say to me?"

Lemon Lady #1 calls back to her as if to offer caring advice but her tone is anything but caring, "It's unhealthy to be so sour all the time. You should try smiling."

"I am smiling...just not at you."

The older Chinese woman snickers at that. Kimi nods at the old woman and exits back into the apartment. The Joy is standing there waiting for her. Fuck. Is this going to be another confrontation? How can she never leave this apartment and still have all of these confrontations?

The Joy smiles. "That was funny."

"What?"

"What you said to the Lemon Lady."

Happy for the lack of drama, Kimi gives a quiet, "Thanks?"

"What you said to her. That's what you should put on a mask."

Kimi laughs. "Yeah. Right."

"I mean it. You're funny. People need funny right now."

Kimi thinks about this. Is it a good idea? "You mean masks with smart-ass sayings? You think people would buy that?"

"Well, you'd make them pretty and all."

"Make them pretty." The Joy's words trigger a flood of design thoughts in Kimi's head. She's thinking it through as she talks, "I could do that. I could, wait, listen. Wait. What if...I kept it pretty, but totally smart-ass. Like I do these scrolling, vine-like designs with the words in lovely lettering that snake around the vines so it's graphic and beautiful and in complete contrast to the crappy sentiments? Is that good?"

The Joy points a knowing finger. "My rule is, if I wake up hung over and still think something is a good idea, then it's a good idea."

Suddenly semi-happy, Kimi asks, "Does that mean we need to start drinking?"

"Oh, my God. Yes!" The Joy hurries into the kitchen. She's so happy. She hates not being liked and that lasted way too long. What would be the right drink to celebrate? Aperol Spritz! Problem solved. She carefully creates the cocktails and joins Kimi on the sofa. Kimi's already got her sketch pad out and is drawing vines. The Joy hands her a cocktail and clinks her glass on Kimi's.

"Cheers." The Joy leans over to Kimi's pad. "What have you got there?"

Kimi tilts the sketch pad so The Joy can see it. There's the outline of a mask. On it, laced through pencil-line, vine art creates scrolling words that say, "No one likes you for a reason." The Joy is delighted. "Oh, I want that one."

"Yeah? Hey, what did I say to that Lemon bitch?...I'm smiling. Just not at you?"

The Joy corrects her, "Not "*I'm. I am.*"

Kimi thinks for a moment then writes it down. "That is better. This is good. Thank you."

"I knew we'd be friends again...How's Carmen?"

"I thought you wanted to be friends."

The Joy thinks for a moment, then, "...So what do you think of Trump's chances for reelection? Can Biden take it?"

"Yes. Let's stick to politics and religion." They clink glasses again and drink.

SHAD & BENJI'S APARTMENT/SHAD'S BEDROOM

Shad is on his bed smelling his socks. They should really be washed. But maybe not. No. They should be washed. He puts them in a hamper in his closet and goes back to his computer. He's watching the scroll when he gets a text from Max. "Call me now." Damn. That was fast. Shad tries to gather his composure. Who's he fooling? This is going to be hard no matter how much composure he has. Although...Christopher said it was easy. Just a "good luck" and that was it. Maybe that will be it. After all, it's just a job opportunity. It's not even in the same city. He's not going to a direct competitor. This happens all the time. People develop and move on from their mentors. It's business. It's not personal. It's just business. OK. Let's do this.

Shad takes a deep breath and calls Max. He gets Max's outgoing message. Shit. He's immediately thrown off his game. What's my message? He just starts talking, "Hey Max. Shad here. But...you knew that. I'm around. Call whenever." He hangs up. Could he have sounded weaker?

STEPH'S APARTMENT

Steph is pacing in front of her window wall. She's on her cell with Bill and excited by what he's asking her. He doesn't sound like he's in the best health, but that's not her initial focus.

Bill continues, "I think you'd be great for it."

Steph catches her reflection and fixes her hair. "Bill, I'm flattered."

"You have a kindness that really comes across. I think that's exactly what's needed here."

"Wow. No one's ever said that."

Enough niceties. Back to business, Bill charges forward. "Listen, this gal is going to be devastated and in shock. And she's going to be worried that she could look like a bad mother. It's your job to put her at ease and just let her tell her story her way. We'll make it usable."

Steph understood. Mrs. Rita Moore, got thrust into the spotlight when her husband was killed overseas. He was a hero who died saving others. And one of the most touching letters home—of all time—was found in his pocket. It was to his wife and kids. She's now left with two sets of twins in a small lower-east side apartment and is currently very pregnant. It's a feel-good, or rather a feel-bad piece. The kind they like to end a news day with. Bill coughs for a good long while. Long enough for Steph to remember that he's been sick. She asks, "How are you feeling?"

"This thing is a real bitch. The doctor says I'll come out of it. Who knows what I'll be left with, but hey, that's what makes life fun, right?"

"Sure. Yeah..." Looking for intel, but trying to sound casual, Steph says, "Hey um, what does Janis say about me getting this story?"

"I'm sure she'll be fine with it. One of her teams is getting a nice break. Why not, right? Bill laughs to himself then adds, "And she needs something in the win column right now after that text thread."

Here comes Steph's intel. She asks, "I'm sorry?"

Through a mixture of coughing and laughing, Bill goes into office gossip mode. "Don't tell me you haven't heard. What kind of news woman are you?" More coughing.

KIMI'S CORNER

Kimi's back in her spot. Did the cocktails give her strength or just drown her fear? Hard to know. She's hoping it's the former. She pulls out her phone and brings up her message thread with Carmen. Best not to read it. She texts, "I think I've had a breakthrough." Now it's her turn to wait for a response. Should she have lead with an apology, or some kind of an explanation? That wouldn't have been her style. Doesn't Carmen want her for her? A few minutes go by, then a few more. She looks at her sketches. Perhaps not.

THE JOY'S APARTMENT

The Joy's hair is back to blond. She escorts a client out of the apartment—
a thirty-something gal with short blond hair that has a fair amount of pink
in it. The gal seems a bit unsure. As she leaves, The Joy says, "I think it
looks good. You can't even tell I've been drinking." The gal disappears.
Right before The Joy closes the door, she sees Vlad with a package for the
apartment across the hall. He sees her.

The Joy raises and eyebrow and uses her seductive tone. "Hey you."

Vlad looks over and smiles.

"Have a package for me?"

SHAD & BENJI'S APARTMENT

Benji has the Wii going when Shad walks though the living room. As he continues his game, he turns to Shad. "Hey. Wanna play?"

Shad's about to turn him down. His head's totally in work and the call from Max that could come any time. But you know what, "Sure. Yeah, I'll play."

Benji is over the moon. He stops his game and turns to Shad, "Wanna play *Mario Karts,* or *Resident Evil*, or *Golf*?

Wanting to build a bridge, Shad offers, "Let's do *Mario Karts*."

Benji thinks, "Could this day get better?" Just then, Douglas/Fluffers jumps onto the sofa. Benji sets up the game play for two players. Shad joins him on the sofa and picks his avatar. Benji asks, "Wanna go first?"

Shad knows that while that sounds like a gift, Benji likes going second so he can see what score he has to beat. Even trying to be a good friend, Benji has his limitations. But, that's okay. "Sure."

Shad starts his *Kart*. But just a few moments into his turn, his cell rings. It's Max. Of course. Shad stops playing and his *Kart* crashes. Sorry bro. I gotta take this." He gets up and heads to his room without looking back. Benji is, once again, alone.

Into his phone, Shad says, "Max. Thanks for getting back to me."

"But first, I made you sweat."

"What?"

"I made you sweat. That's why I didn't call you back right away. You deserved to sweat."

After a long moment, Shad chooses to ignore the sweat conversation and just go straight to the point. He tells himself to be strong. "Max, I want to tell you how much I've appreciated everything you've taught me. But I'm going to be accepting an offer at..."

Max interrupts, "No, you're not."

"You didn't even hear what I was going to say."

"Doesn't matter. You're not going to South Carolina. South Carolina is bullshit."

"The entire state?"

"Listen to me. It's a wrong move."

What the hell? Shad asks, "Didn't you congratulate Christopher on the new job? Didn't you wish him well?"

"I did and I do. But not you."

"Why not me?"

"Are you really buying into that big fish, small pond bullshit? Wouldn't you rather be a big fish in a big pond?"

Shad's thrown, "Well..."

"Things got hard for a minute. Maybe you thought I wasn't a *nice guy*. Boo-hoo. Nice is bullshit. You don't need nice. You're young, you're living in New York City, and you're a gunslinger. You forgot your guns for a second. Fine. Move on. At this point in the game, all we need to do is show up to make money. I hired you because you're an A-type, with an athlete's mentality who gets shit done. Well, get shit done. Find a finish line and cross it. Then find the next finish line and cross that. Want to know why I wished Christopher well?" He doesn't wait for an answer. "Because that's the right move for him. Not you. His girl's there. He's not looking to crush it. But you? Big fish, small pond. Looks pretty good, right? Pretty cush. You know how good that's gonna look to you in a year? When you see how much I've crushed it and you weren't a part of it? You're gonna be kicking yourself for not swimming in the big pond. You think I'm not nice? Fuck nice. You're being a total dick to yourself. You're the one selling yourself short. Not me. I'm fighting *for* you. And it's your damn fight. So fight it. Are you a big-pond guy or not? I'll keep you on this team and forget we ever had this conversation, but you have to decide right now. The offer goes away in sixty-seconds. Clock's ticking."

Shad thinks, Jesus! That was part preacher, part father, part coach. His head's spinning.

Max interrupts Shad's confusion, "Thirty-five seconds. Tick, tick, tick."

THE JOY'S APARTMENT

Kimi is in the living room by herself. She looks to make sure that The Joy is nowhere in sight. When she deems the coast clear, she switches the location of two items of juju. A blue marble egg and a plastic strip of bacon that are both sitting on the same china plate. There. Maybe that will change her energy for the good. She looks around, not really expecting a change, but you never know. Nope. No change.

Then she feels her phone vibrate. It's a text from Carmen. [Countless poop emojis.] Well she could count them, but that would change nothing. Kimi puts the items of juju back in their original spots and looks around again. Nothing. After ten minutes, still nothing.

STEPH'S APARTMENT

With a somewhat better outlook, Steph has given herself license to take a break. No work. No workout. She's stretched out on the sofa with a bag of chips, baked not fried, and a book. A real book with pages you can touch and everything. She'd been in a book club with friends from the gym, but had to drop out because she never had time to finish the books and they all gave her shit about, "Maybe you just don't have time for things like friends." Steph thinks, sorry if my career matters to me. You try doing everything that I do, then get back to me. Well, screw them. I'm reading a book. And I picked it myself. It's not that mindless bodice-ripping garbage you all read. Then she realizes that she's not actually reading. Just thinking about reading.

She grabs the remote, rolls to her right and clicks on the TV. There's Ray standing outside yet another closed landmark of a restaurant, reporting that it's shuttered for good. Is that...Shit. That's Little Odessa. Out loud and to no one Steph says, "Ray, you suck...And your tie and mask clash." She turns off the TV.

Steph pulls out her phone and calls Ida.

Ida answers quickly, "What's wrong?"

"You don't want to talk to me?"

"I always want to talk to you. Do you want to Zoom?"

Not wanting to get off the sofa, Steph says, "No. Let's just keep it old-school and just talk."

"Whatever you want. Now, what's wrong?"

"Nothing's wrong. Why does something always have to be wrong. I'm just, I don't know, bored?"

"So you thought you'd call your old mother. Did you ever think that I might be in the middle of something and too busy to talk?"

"Are you?"

"What do I have to do? Of course not."

"Hey, I got a great assignment. I'm going to be interviewing Mary Moore, the woman who..."

Ida cuts in, "The husband died and all those kids. I know. So sad. That's why we only had one child."

"Because you were afraid that Dad would get blown up? I thought that you didn't have more kids because you couldn't have more kids."

Tossing off the truth, Ida says, "Potato, tomato...Congratulations on your story. You'll tell me when to watch. Are you ever going to do a story on your aunt's challah?"

Steph gives an abrupt, "No."

"Fine. Sorry I asked."

Steph wants to get away from challah talk as quickly as possible. "New topic. Mother's Day is coming up. I thought I could bring something special for dinner."

"Oh, honey, no. We don't want you coming here right now."

Steph is completely taken aback. "What do you mean?"

"Well, you go out, and you're with all those people, and touching things. Your father and I just think it would be better if you didn't come right now."

Steph can't believe how incredibly sad she is at hearing this. But she gets it. Her parents are older than most of her friends' parents and fall into the at-risk category. She's been seeing firsthand how this virus is effecting everything. She's not fooling herself. She just never thought about not being able to see them. This is so messed up. "Oh, OK. Yeah, that makes complete sense."

"You're disappointed."

With a stiff upper lip, Steph lets Ida off the hook. "Of course I am. But I understand and I think you guys are right. I'll come down when things start clearing up."

"OK. Well, you'll let us know when your interview is going to be on so we can tell everyone to watch. Marge Belchek's son had a story in the neighborhood paper and we all had to hear about it for weeks. You are much more impressive than he is and I plan to not shut up about this for months. Screw Marge Belchek!"

"Screw Marge Belchek!"

"Love you, baby."

"Love you, too. Love to Dad."

Ida hangs up. Steph feel worse than when she was merely bored. Now she's bored and sad. After a moment, she sends Jackson a text. "You at home [wink emoji]?"

SHAD & BENJI'S APARTMENT

Benji is in the kitchen. Mixing bowls are everywhere. He's got a bowl in one hand and is mixing with the other like he's on a mission. Can't stop mixing. Must keep mixing. He knows he's stuck in a spiral, but can't break the pattern. At least things are getting well mixed.

KIMI'S CORNER

Kimi is in her regular garb, with the addition of a big, red winter hat. Why? It's May. But the hat feels bizarrely comforting around her head. It's become her new work/thinking hat. She's loading her new designs onto her website. Each new mask sports a sarcastic saying subtly incorporated into a floral design. She admires the work. She likes the smartass attitude. Will anyone else? No, it's good. But she needs a better name for the line. Without any more thought than that, she clicks on GoDaddy to see if *InYourFaceMasks* is available. She can hear a drum roll in her head as she waits to see if it's taken. It has to be taken. It's too obvious. Holy Shit! It's available. *InYourFaceMasks.* Buy it. Hurry! Buy it! Done. She sits backs feeling like she's just had her first triumph in a long damn time. No, it's not a homerun...yet. But it feels right.

Her next thought is that she wants to share this moment with someone. She thinks about Carmen. Fuck.

JACKSON'S APARTMENT

Jackson is out on the balcony. He's sitting cross-legged on top of a large, glass-top table with a beautiful tray of food on his lap. Different cheeses, nuts and lots of colorful fruit. He absently eats as he looks out over his quiet city. He then checks out his biceps. Better. He's made nice progress. He's pleased with his dedication. He thinks, "See, I can stick to something." Who knows when *Ninja Warrior* will be able to return, but he's going to be ready.

Now, what's going to be the emotional story of helping others that gets him on? It's got to be big. It can't just be one donation. He thinks, "What's a cause that matters to me? What do I care about?" How could this much nothing come to mind? People are sick. People are hungry. Sure, he feels bad about those things, but does he really feel it? Not really. It's not personal. It's all too far away. Nothing hits close to home. Why is this so hard? "Keep thinking."

In the distance, he can hear the door buzzer. He calls out, "Can you get that?"

A woman's voice with little expression says, "Stay put, Jacky. Don't put yourself out."

SHAD & BENJI'S APARTMENT/SHAD'S BEDROOM

Shad's pacing energetically in his room. He's charged. He's pumped. He's made a decision. He's emboldened. He thinks, "This is me. I'm back. I'm a winner. I know this guy. I like this guy." He's ready to take responsibility for his life again. "What else?" His work direction is solved...as much as it can ever be. It's a moving target, but he now feels like he can keep pace and move with it.

But now he wants something else—something that's all him. He's an athlete. He's always been an athlete. Even when he didn't stick with football, he still ran track. He needs a finish line. He feels like he's going to burst out of his skin. "God, this room is small." He gets up on his bed and starts running in place. "What next?" The bouncing is helping to slow his mind down. He can think. He wonders, "Is this what Benji feels? Does the rhythm of repeated movement calm him down?" So much clarity.

There's a knock on his door. Shad calls out, "What?" He didn't mean to sound shitty. It just came out that way. Not doing his usual, thoughtless bust in, Benji talks through the door. "Can I come in?"

Shad stops running, but stays on the bed. "Sure."

Benji pushes open the door. He's holding a pie. Without being fazed in any way that Shad is standing on his bed, Benji says, "I made you a Boston Cream Pie, even though it's really cake."

Shad quietly negates him. "Dude, it's pie."

"It's cake."

They stare at each other. Shad gives. He likes Benji. The guy just frustrates him sometimes. A lot of the time. It's not really his fault. Shad asks, "Why?"

Answering the wrong question, Benji replies, "Because it's two pieces of cake with cream in the middle. The pie tin is irrelevant."

"No, man. Why did you make it?"

"Felt bad."

"You should...Give me the pie."

Benji steps up onto Shad's bed. He pulls two forks out of his back pocket and offers one to Shad. Shad takes the fork then goes in for a big bite. He exclaims, "God damn, that's not right!"

Worried, Benji asks, "No good?"

"So good."

They both stand on the bed delighting in what Benji created. Benji interrupts the indulgent flavor bliss, "I decided to rename my sourdough 'Fluffers.' The name came available."

Shad smiles, "Cool. And...it's pie."

"Cake."

THE JOY'S APARTMENT/BEDROOM

The Joy has her armoire open. She's digging through an amount of clothing that doesn't seem possible to be able to fit in the old piece of furniture. Kimi comes to the door. From her angle, it looks like The Joy is being swallowed by chiffon. She watches for a while before The Joy notices that she's there and says, "Oh. Hey. I wasn't expecting company."

Not expecting an answer, Kimi asks, "Got enough chiffon there?"

The Joy catches on. "Oh, you think I have too much. I get it."

"I'm just saying, maybe something khaki to break it up."

The Joy pauses. And wonders how could someone think that anyone *needs* khaki. Then, "That was a joke."

"It was, indeed."

The Joy has no idea why Kimi's there and Kimi doesn't feel like starting the conversation, but we can't always get what we want, can we? So Kimi finally shares, "I got a new name for my business." The Joy waits for more information. Kimi thinks, "Christ, why can't she just ask? Why is she making me do all the work? Fine." She says, "It's called, In Your Face Masks."

Another long pause.

The Joy smiles. "That's amazing!"

Relieved and happy to share her minor success with someone, Kimi says, "Well, maybe not *amazing*."

"No. It's amazing. That's really good. Way better than I thought you were going to do. I thought you'd do something like, *On* Your Face Masks, which is a little too lesbo for me...Oh, sorry. Too soon?"

"It's fine. I totally deserve that. And, I think I like *On Your Face* even better. Wait. Do I?...I do. But you do like it?" Kimi knew that The Joy was being sincere, but she selfishly craved a little more praise.

"Oh, yeah."

Kimi shifts focus to all the fabric trying to fight its way out of the armoire. "How do you find anything?"

"I know. Right?"

Kimi walks over and takes a good long look in. That's madness. She carefully says, "Maybe you should *consider*...getting rid of some things?"

"It's just so hard to say goodbye to friends."

Kimi holds up a particularly loud garment. "Need a hand?"

Suddenly excited, The Joy says, "Yes. I need someone to be tough with me...Too soon?"

Smiling, Kimi says, "Fuck you."

Together they start going through The Joy's ridiculous supply of body coverings. Before long, they start to create a system. Things go into one of four piles; keep, donate, burn, costume. The costume pile is also a keep pile, but with a different intent. As they make their way through the armoire, Kimi is seeing that the donate and burn piles are not getting a lot of love. "You are going to have to part with something."

"I know. I know. This is just harder than I thought."

"Suck it up, Buttercup...too soon?" They both laugh, each of them realizing that they hadn't laughed together in longer than either could remember. It feels good.

As the laughter dies down, The Joy asks, "We're good, right?"

"We're good."

The Joy goes to hug Kimi, but Kimi pulls back saying, "No touching."

The Joy smiles then sees the clock on her bed-side table. She turns to Kimi." Look at the time. We're minutes from video cocktails and I've done absolutely nothing about our drinks."

Looking at all of the clothing on the floor, Kimi says, "We're not done. What are you going to do with all this?"

The Joy looks at her piles of wearable treasures on the floor, scoops them up and shoves the entire lot back into the armoire.

"What are you doing?!"

"You didn't really think I was going to throw my clothes away, did you?"

"Actually, I did."

"No. I was just letting you re-bond with me." With that, The Joy leaves Kimi standing in her bedroom. Kimi realizes she's just been outsmarted by The Joy. Wow, she must really be slipping.

ZOOM-A-ZOOM-A-ZOOM

THE JOY'S APARTMENT

Kimi follows the Joy into the living room. The Joy is heading straight for the kitchen counter. She's on a mission. Kimi enters. "You suck, you know that?"

Deep in her task, The Joy replies, "The better to see you with, my dear."

That made no sense. Correction. It made "The Joy sense," which is no sense except to The Joy. Kimi decides to not address it and take this very strange moment of peace to enjoy it. She will let this woman make her a drink...that she doesn't have to pay for...with money...and let her friends share their stories that, with any luck, will be worse than hers. Wouldn't that be nice?

The Joy is finishing with her cocktail prep and explains, "I'm making New York sours. It's like a Whiskey sour, but with a red wine float. One glass. Two drinks. What genius thought of that one! I assume you want one."

"Assume away."

The Joy remarks, "Nice-Kimi is so much more fun, don't you agree?" The Joy hands Kimi a rocks glass filled to the rim. Then, new inspiration hits. She turns the computer 180 degrees and brings her stool to the other side of the counter. She motions for Kimi to join her.

"What are you doing?"

"You and I are keeping it fresh. New background for the gang. Come on." Kimi brings her stool around as The Joy logs into the video call. They watch their friends once again fumble with the settings to turn on their audio and video. It's painful to watch every time.

Kimi:" Really. How long have we been doing this?" She then remembers that her plan was to be relaxed and maybe not so abrasive...Fuck it. Go with your strength.

Finally, The Joy holds up her glass. Everyone on the call follows suit. With a flourish, she says, "I declare this week's cocktail call officially open."

Kimi sees that everyone has virtually identical drinks. "Wait, are we all drinking the same thing?"

Jackson, looking like he just had a rather pleasant workout interjects, "The Joy emailed the recipe. I do as told."

Kimi: "I didn't get an email."

The Joy: "It was on a need-to-know basis. Also...I'd like to announce that Kimi and I have re-bonded...in case you noticed that things have been a little on the chilly side over here."

Everyone over-talks their own version of, "What? No..."

Benji: "And Shad and I are all good, too."

Shad: "He made me a pie."

Benji: "Cake."

Kimi turns to The Joy, "I didn't get a pie."

The Joy: "You'll get booze and like it."

Finally noticing that they're down a man, The Joy says, "Wait, where's Steph?" Everyone looks around as if she's going to pop up on someone's screen. Nothing.

The Joy: "This is unacceptable."

Just then another window joins the call. It's Steph. She looks like a large wind has just blown in the door. She still has her bag over her shoulder, and a glass and unopened wine bottle in her hand. She's breathless. "Sorry I'm late. Sorry, sorry."

The Joy: "This is unacceptable."

Steph: "I just gave you three sorrys. What have I missed?"

The Joy is visibly put out. "Oh, my God. So much. Kimi and I have re-bonded, not that anyone noticed, Shad and Benji exchanged a pie..."

Benji: "Cake."

The Joy: "Whatever."

Steph: "Wow. I did miss a lot. Well, I have big news. Huge. You will not believe this shit. I mean, you can't make this stuff up. Seriously."

Annoyed, The Joy says, "I guess you have the floor."

Responding formally, Steph says, "Thank you The Joy. Now...what...a...week! First, I wasn't getting any assignments and I thought I was going to be fired for God knows what. I told you all that. Then I got a huge assignment and my boss, Janis, is getting fired! Seriously. Can you believe it? Fired."

Shad: "Janis is out?"

Steph: "Out. Now, ask me why?"

Kimi: "Why?"

Steph: "Glad you asked. First, Janis is stonewalling me because she thinks I was telling everyone about her private life, which she dumps into my lap daily. I mean, I have to listen to some seriously crazy shit. Did you know that she had her girlfriend move in, made her sequester in a tiny guest bedroom for two weeks and then, then it turns out that the chick's kid is in the tiny guest room, too? No. Of course you didn't, because I don't talk out of turn. Then I find out from Bill, who it looks like will survive COVID, thank God, who it was that *actually* told everyone about Janis's crazy escapades. Guess who told. Guess."

Shad: "You know we don't know your coworkers."

Steph: "Guess."

Jackson: "I like Anderson Cooper. I guess him."

Steph pauses at that odd response. "OK, I'll tell you. It was…Janis! Janis told everyone about Janis 'stupid life. Apparently, she and her girlfriend had a *huge* blow up. And Janis put a cherry on it with a night of drunk texting. How much do you love that?"

Kimi: "That's good."

Steph:" So good. And, there's more. She went on some ageist rant about Bill. She literally said that he was too old and addled to be doing his job anymore and that his getting COVID only sped up what was coming anyway."

Shad: "Holy shit."

Steph: "Right?! Wait, I need to read you just a little bit of this. Oh my shit, this is so good! OK…" She does her best drunk Janis impersonation. "'What a bitch!!!' Three exclamation points! 'Where's the loyalty?' Question mark! 'And that kid!!!' Three exclamation points! 'This is not because I'm drunk.' Five wine glass emojis! 'Which I fucking am!!!' Three exclamation points! 'Is Bill dead yet?!!!' Question mark! Three exclamation points!" Back in her own voice Steph says, "It seems that the magic number for exclamation points is three."

Shad: "You said she got fired, right?"

Steph: "So fired…And there's more! Bill gave me a seriously great assignment. I'm interviewing…Rita Moore. Captain Moore's widow."

Benji: "The one with the twins?"

Steph: "Correct."

The Joy: "You are forgiven."

Steph: "Thank you. And cheers to me." Steph raises her glass and everyone else follows. All say, "Cheers."

The Joy: "And our Kimi here has some news, too."

Steph: "Really?"

Kimi's suddenly uncomfortable in the spotlight.: "It's nothing."

Steph: "Spill it."

The Joy: "I'll spill. Our Kimi has a beautiful, new line of masks with her wonderful smartass sayings, and guess what it's called?"

No one says anything.

The Joy: "So you'll guess for Steph and not for me?"

Shad: "Kimi's Mean Girl Masks."

The Joy: "No."

Benji: "Mrs. Mask Maiden."

The Joy: "No. That's kind of awful. OK, I'll tell you. They're called, On Your Face Masks."

The name is well received. Everyone voices their sincere approval.

The Joy: "Kimi, tell them about it. No, wait. Show them."

Reluctant but proud, Kimi gets her laptop. She brings up the site and shows the gang a few of her designs and reads the sarcastic sayings buried in the art. "This one says, *I don't know you but I hate you.* This one says, *Would a breath mint kill you?* This one says, *Yes, your mask makes your ass look fat.*"

Excitedly, Benji chimes in, "Oh, you could make masks that have a line down the middle and call them, Ass Face Masks."

Everyone stops to think about that. Did Benji just have a good idea? Kimi picks up the ball, "I like that. I think I could do it as a line extension. Really simple. Subtle. Thanks, Mr. B. If you have any more of those ideas, let me know. I'll cut you in." Benji sits up straighter and turns to Shad. Shad toasts him in approval.

Jackson: "I have an idea. What if you did a mask with a hole in it? Like for straws...And, and, you could eat French fries through it?"

Kimi actively ignores Jackson's idea. "So Benji, you keep those ideas coming."

Jackson: "Fine. It's a good idea."

Kimi: "It's not."

Steph: "Kimi, I wish you well in your venture."

Kimi: "Thank you."

Steph: "Shad, did I miss any news about you?"

Shad: "What kind of news?"

The Joy: "Oh, that's right. Are you abandoning your very best friends from high school?"

Shad: "We were *not* best friends in high school."

The Joy: "And now I guess we know why."

Shad: "No. I'm not leaving."

The Joy: "Hey, the band is back together!"

Shad: "I never left the band."

The Joy: "Mentally you did. And we were great friends in high school. Except I didn't hang out with Steph...or Jackson...or you."

Kimi: "Great friends."

Benji: "Remember that time when we snuck out at lunch to get cheese fries at Big John's? Jackson, you made me think of it when you said French fries."

Kimi: "I remember that breaking the rules almost made you shit your pants."

Benji: "There's a significant line between almost shitting your pants and actually shitting them. I went."

Steph: "Was I there?"

Kimi: "No. You didn't like us."

Steph: "I liked you. We just traveled in different circles."

Kimi: "Yes, beautiful, cool circles and strange, misunderstood circles."

Jackson: "For what it's worth, I think we are all cool."

The Joy: "Thank you."

Benji: "...and I can too break rules."

Kimi: "Really? Prove it."

Benji thinks. "OK...Yes...I got a box delivered this week and I never wiped it down." He turns to Shad. "Sorry, man."

Shad: "Forgiven."

Steph: "Wow. You *are* a daredevil."

Benji: "What, not daring enough for the cool kids?" Benji gets up and leaves the frame. Shad shrugs to the others as if to say he has no idea what his roommate is up to.

After a moment, Benji reenters with an opened box. "This is it. This is the box my mom used to send cookies."

Shad: "I didn't get cookies."

To Shad, Benji says, "We didn't like each other back then." He turns to the group, "But watch this!" Benji licks the box.

The entire gang recoils at this stunt. There's a round of, "No! Don't do that! Oh, my God! Benji, stop. No!"

Benji: "I dare you all."

Kimi: "You want us to lick your box?" As an aside to The Joy, Kimi says, "Too soon?" They laugh.

Benji: "I dare you all to lick something."

Steph: "That's disgusting."

Benji: "Scared? I think the person who licks the most unsafe thing wins."

Kimi: "Wins what?"

Benji: "A dollar."

Kimi: "I honestly liked your Ass Face idea way better."

Jackson: "I'll do it."

Steph: "No. Don't lick..."

Jackson: "Wait. wait. I need to think...Wait. OK. Simple. Got it."

Jackson pulls off one of his Nike flip flops and licks it. The gang groans.

Benji: "Seriously gross, dude."

Jackson: "Thank you. I want my dollar."

Steph: "I can't look at you."

Trying to egg Steph on, The Joy teases, "You don't want to kiss your boyfriend?"

Steph: "What? What are you talking about? He's not my boyfriend."

Kimi: "Fuck buddy?"

Steph: "Seriously Kimi? I hate that phrase."

The Joy: "Come on. You can tell us...Oh, I have an idea, let's all share a secret."

Steph: "Let's not."

Shad: "I have one."

The Joy: "Yay!"

Shad: "I'm going to run a marathon."

Steph: "What? Where?"

Shad: "Right here, in the apartment. And I'm making Benji here my wingman." Benji is delighted at the news. Everyone else is perplexed.

Kimi: "Wait. No. You are going to run an entire marathon, twenty-six point three miles, in a cramped, New York apartment?"

Shad: "I am."

Kimi: "Why?"

Shad: "I need a purpose. I need to accomplish something—something besides work.

Jackson: "I completely understand. If there's anything I can do to help, let me know."

Shad: "Thanks, man"

Jackson: "You bet."

The Joy: "Wow. I feel like we really got a lot done today."

Shad: "I guess you're done with us."

The Joy: "I have to see a man about a horse."

Steph: "I'm going to text all of you the info so you can watch my interview."

Benji: "OK. Wingman, signing out."

Kimi: "Wait. Wait—www dot on your face masks dot com. Buy one. Tell your friends."

The Joy: "And we all have to share a secret next time."

That announcement is followed by groans and goodbyes...And they're gone.

GETTING GOOD AT THIS

SHAD & BENJI'S APARTMENT

Benji's on the sofa with Douglas. *Mind Of A Chef* is on the TV. Benji watches intently. He's seen all the David Chang episodes at least three times. He's now watching a Sean Brock episode...again, and thinking about how he could get his hands on some Carolina heritage rice. Delivery to the city has been so hit or miss. He feels his phone vibrate and sees he has a text from Patrick, reading, "Great news. Call me." While still watching his show, Benji hits the call button.

Patrick: "Dude, great news. It was a tough sell but I got the guys to agree to let you move in. I mean, the rent is going up a little from what Pete was paying, but he was one of the originals. Just makes sense, right? But hey, great news, right?"

Without much effort in his words, Benji says, "No thanks."

Patrick sounds surprised at being turned down. "What? Is it the money?"

"No."

Almost in a plead, Patrick explains, "But I went to bat for you, man."

"I don't need it. I can stay where I am."

"What if we keep it to what Pete was paying?"

"I don't need it."

Dejected, Patrick laments, "This sucks, man. No one's working. No one can afford the rent. This sucks."

Benji's apathetic. It's not his problem anymore. His TV show is way more interesting. With little energy he gets out a, "Yeah."

Half out loud, half to himself, Patrick says, "Fuck. If I have to move back in with my mother...Fuck." He hangs up. Benji stays in his food-show trance.

THE JOY'S APARTMENT

Kimi has on her make-it-happen, red winter hat, and is carrying her laptop and a plate of rice and beans. She walks across the living room and stops at the windowsill. How the hell is she going to maneuver this? Puzzles. Puzzles. OK, break it down. She balances everything precariously on the arm of an upholstered chair, then opens the window. She carefully reaches her plate over the juju and onto the fire escape, turns, grabs her laptop right before it slides off the arm and onto the floor. Kimi tucks the laptop under her arm, steps onto the chair and then over the juju onto the fire escape while trying to not step into her lunch. Next, she lowers herself slowly into place. Kimi looks around as if expecting applause. Nothing. Wait. She looks up and sees Baby Mom clapping for her. Kimi raises a hand to the not-so-stranger. Nice.

There's the sound of a siren in the distance. It doesn't throw her like it had in the beginning of lockdown. In the beginning, every siren made her stop what she was doing and worry about the impending doom. Now, she just opens up her computer and clicks to her website. While it's coming up, she grabs her plate and takes a fork full of food. Checking for mask sales on her website has become her new version of checking her lottery numbers. And...eight! Eight sales. Holy shit! Could she be more delighted? Well, yeah. Eight hundred would be more delightful. But eight. Yes. Eight is the luckiest number for Chinese people. Not that she believes in that shit. She says the Chinese word for "eight" in her head. It sounds like the Chinese word for wealth. She thinks, This is right. This is going to happen. She's sure that the next time she checks, the number will be a multiple of eight which is even luckier. Not that she believes in that shit.

SHAD & BENJI'S APARTMENT/SHAD'S BEDROOM

Shad is sitting at his computer dressed for work. He's finishing off a "checking-in" email for a client. In general, he's switched from checking-in emails to checking-in calls, but some people, like Mr. Undermint, would rather have the email. Bonus...with emails, there's a record, so he can always have backup if something's questioned. Done.

He looks at the time on his computer. Lunch. Shad pushed back, gets up and starts to undress. He puts on shorts and a tech top. From under the bed he pulls out a box with a new pair of Hoka running shoes. He figured the extra cushion would be helpful on his treadmill as well as the unforgiving apartment floor. Why is putting on a brand-new pair of running shoes so exciting? It's like the promise of achievement. He puts them on and starts stretching. He thinks, "I can do this. I will do this."

THE JOY'S APARTMENT/FIRE ESCAPE

As she enjoys the concert of random sounds around her neighborhood, Kimi finishes her beans and rice. Was that so good because she's hyped up from selling a few masks or was it just that good? She looks around. No one's watching her. She licks the plate.

JACKSON'S APARTMENT/HALLWAY

Jackson's dressed for Ninja training. He's got music that's designed to pump him up pounding over two small speakers that sit on the floor. The newest addition to his home-course is now five strips of wood screwed onto the wall. They're not quite end-to-end. There are gaps between them of various distances. The idea is to grab onto a narrow strip and travel the wall while hanging from your fingers. In front of him is a mini-tramp. He readies himself, then bounces up to the first strip. He begins his trek, hand over hand, sideways down the hall. His fingers feel strong. He gets to the end of the first strip and reaches across the gap to the second strip. Success. But then, one of the screws pulls from the wall, the strip comes undone and Jackson is on his ass. Shit!

A woman's voice calls out, "What did you break?"

Jackson, staring up at the wall, calls back, "I'm fine."

STEPH'S APARTMENT

Steph is surfing the web. *The Morning Show* from Apple TV plays on one of her screens. She's also on the phone with Ida, who's going on about some neighbor. Something Steph knows that she's heard before. She thinks, "God I love *The Morning Show*. I could be Jennifer Aniston. It's not so crazy."

Ida asks, "Are you even listening?"

Steph feigns an interest in Ida's ramblings. "Of course I'm listening. You have my undivided attention... Now can you say that again?"

"I said that your father doesn't listen and neither do you.

"I'm sorry, Mom. Just say it again."

"Why don't you tell me something. I'm tired of hearing myself talk."

"OK, tell dad that you guys need to watch the five o'clock news tomorrow. I'm doing my interview with Mrs. Moore in the morning and it's going up on the five o'clock."

Ida asks, "What are you going to wear?"

"I'm not sure yet. I'll find something."

"I know what you have. You have nothing."

"Oh, my God, Mom...How about the orange top and the gray skirt?"

"Who raised you? Wear the blue."

Steph thinks about that. "The blue blouse?"

Ida's definitive." The dark blue, not the teal. And the copper pencil skirt. Everyone looks amazing in a pencil skirt."

Steph considers this. Say what you will, Ida knows how to put an outfit together. "Thanks, Mom."

"You're very welcome. Now, go back to your life and leave me alone."

Steph smiles. "Love you, Mom. Love to Dad."

"Love you, too."

"They both hang up. Jennifer Aniston pulls Steph's attention again. Steph thinks, "Here I come." Steph picks her phone up again and texts the gang. "I'm on the 5 p.m. news tomorrow. Watch. I know you'll be home."

THE JOY'S APARTMENT

The Joy, wearing one of Kimi's masks, is walking Mr. Simon, a short round man, to the door. It's hard to tell why he needed an appointment with The Joy. He has about three hairs on his head. But he's pleasant and clearly happy with the experience.

As a form of goodbye, The Joy semi-sings, "OK, Mr. Simon."

"Please, call me Ambrose."

"I can't. You look like my high school algebra teacher. It's conditioning." Mr. Simon shrugs sweetly, puts on his Yankees cap and walks out. As he heads down the hall, The Joy calls after him, "I got an A in algebra." Without turning back, he raises his hand in recognition of what she said.

As he leaves, he holds open the front door of the building for Vlad. Vlad heads right to The Joy. The Joy grabs a mask off the top of the sideboard by the door. There's now a small stack of them there on a tray. "Hey there. I have something for you." The Joy hands a mask to Vlad. It's one of Kimi's designs.

Vlad, clearly happy to see her, hands The Joy an envelope. "And I have something for you."

They exchange their gifts. The Joy says, "Read it."

Vlad holds up the mask and sees that buried in the scrolling design it says, "I'd rather have something else on my face." He smiles and puts it on over his PackageGuys mask.

The Joy purrs, "Ohh. Now, you're extra safe."

Vlad smiles, not that The Joy can see it, and gestures to the envelope he just handed her. "Read yours."

She opens the cardboard envelope in as sexy a manner as she can muster. It's actually not that sexy, but they both enjoy the intent. She pulls out the official-looking letter and reads it. And with that, all pretense at sexy drains from her face.

SHAD & BENJI'S APARTMENT

Shad and Benji are prepping for a rare, eat-dinner-at-the-table evening. The prep involves Shad sitting at the table and waiting for Benji to serve him. While Benji finishes his work in the kitchen, Shad thinks about how maybe this is what it's like to be in a relationship. When you get mad at each other, you hang in, and then you work it out. And then you get a fantastic, make-up dinner. He feels like he's just had a revelation and that perhaps he's growing as a person. He's impressed with himself.

Shad's lost in his self-aggrandizing thoughts as Benji places a plate in front of him. It's poached salmon over a bed of quinoa with a lightly sautéed vegetable medley on the side. Beautiful and healthy. Shad is impressed with the offering. "That looks amazing."

As Benji places another plate down for himself, he sits and says formally, "You are most welcome. What you have in front of you is salmon poached in white wine and the vegetables sautéed in lemon and olive oil. No butter. It's all on your training plan. I would have poured a nice Chablis that I have cellared under my bed, but I figured you're not drinking."

Shad digs in. He wants to wait and not talk with his mouth full, but *damn*. "That is so good."

"You like it?"

"Hell yeah."

They both dig in and keep eating without saying a word until all signs of food are gone. Shad sits back and puts his hands behind his head. He just nods in approval. After a pause, Benji smiles, picks up both of their empty plates and takes them to the sink.

Shad calls to him, "Just leave 'em in the sink. I'll do it. I just want to sit here for a sec and think about that."

Unbothered, Benji calls back, "I'll do it."

"No, man. I'll get to it." Shad knows that his words are just a gesture. Benji's happy to do it and Shad's happy to let him. He decides to throw Benji a bone. He calls out over the sound of running water, "Hey, wanna watch *Galaxy Quest*?"

With sci-fi excitement in the air, Benji turns off the water. "You have to love the classics. No. Wait. No. We should watch *Never Surrender*. It's the making-of *Galaxy Quest*. You have to see the part about the Thermians. How they clap? So good."

Shad shrugs. "Fine."

Benji leaves the kitchen to set up their night of geeky fun. He manages the movie on his iPad and sets it so they can watch it on the TV. Shad comes to the sofa. Inspiration strikes. "Think we'll need popcorn?"

Benji is so in. "Oh, we definitely need popcorn." He gets up and heads back to the kitchen. He calls back, "You finish ordering the movie. I'm on the popcorn. Hey, I'm thinking, Old Bay Spice."

"I like how you think."

"I know you don't. But that's OK."

Wow. Shad wonders how separate Benji feels from everyone else. Benji is always such a complicated puzzle. He feels for his friend. The sound of his phone pulls him out of his thoughts. Both Shad and Benji recognize "I'm Too Sexy" as Jackson's ring tone. Shad answers. "Yeah, man."

Jackson greets him, "Shad, my brother from another mother."

"What's up? We were about to watch a movie."

"What's playing?"

"We're going to watch…" Shad calls back to Benji, "What are we watching?"

Benji calls back, *"Never Surrender."*

Back into the phone, Benji says, *"Never Surrender."*

"Oh. That's on my list!"

"Wait. I'm putting you on speaker. "Shad hits the button and asks the obligatory, "Can you hear me?"

"Yes. Yes. I want to watch that. Let's have a watch party."

Benji calls to Jackson. "Cool. You need to make yourself popcorn. I'm making ours with Old Bay."

"Lovely. Before the movie, Shad, I had an idea for your marathon."

Happy for any interest in his venture, Shad says, "Spill it."

"What if…it wasn't just you? What if it was bigger than you?"

Shad doesn't get where this is going. "Dude, it's a small apartment."

"No. I mean, what if other people run a marathon virtually…in their own apartments, or homes, or yards, but at the same time. And…and they pay to do it?"

"You want to monetize my marathon?"

"Yes! No. Not for us. For charity. We get as many people as possible to run a marathon in their homes—at the same time—and all of the money goes to charity." Jackson waits for a response to what he believes to be a genius concept.

Shad lets the idea sink in. The more he thinks about it, the more the possibilities build. This could be big. He feels the gravity of his purpose growing. "It's brilliant."

Pleased, Jackson asks, "You like it?"

"Man, I love it. What's the charity?"

"I haven't gotten that far."

With zero strain of thought, Benji matter-of-factly calls out, "It's for all of the out-of-work restaurant workers."

Shad turns to him. "Did you just think of that?"

Benji shrugs. "It's simple math."

Jackson's thrilled. "It's genius. Are we all good with that?"

"I'm great with it." After his initial enthusiasm, Shad starts to really think about doing this. It's a lot. "Dude, this is not my wheelhouse. Like, how do we get the word out? How do we manage the money? Do we need to set up a non-profit? What's the date? I need time to train. I want a good finish time."

Jackson grabs an, elegant, leather-bound datebook. "I've done some preliminary digging into how to set it. Also, it has to happen fast. Soon. Before someone else does it. People have too much time to think right now and we have to be first to stay relevant. Before everyone is tired of supporting people less fortunate. Pretty soon everyone is going to feel like the less fortunate."

Shad's taken aback. When did Jackson become thoughtful? "So when are you thinking?"

"May 26th."

"Too soon. That's impossible." Shad can't see that working. "I can't train for a marathon in a few weeks."

Jackson had anticipated Shad's response and has an answer ready. "It's not a few weeks. I know you. You've never stopped training. You've been running. You're always ready for a starting gun. And there are tons of people, just like you, who haven't stopped training either. And they're likely ready to climb out of their skin. They'll jump on this thing."

Benji adds, "And...we have everyone video their race. Then we can edit it all together and use the video to raise more money and inspire other races."

Admiring his roommate, Shad remarks, "Smell Wingman!"

Jackson praises his friend. "Shad, look what you started."

Shad can't deny that Jackson's compliment felt good. He's feeling good about all of them. "Bud, look at you. No offense man, but I never saw this side of you coming."

"You're not supposed to...Listen to me. The 26th is the day after Memorial Day. There's going to be nothing else going on. People will log in."

Benji snickers, "You said log."

Shad shakes his head. "You're a child."

Jackson presses on. "Everyone will be looking for a diversion from boredom, right? It's still May, so it's not too hot yet in the city..."

Shad looks concerned. "Still, I think we could push it back a *few* weeks."

"...And it's my father's birthday."

Enough said. Shad acquiesces. "Done."

"I thank you."

"No, thank you. This is exciting. Good thing my chef's watching my intake."

Benji comes over with popcorn and two beers. "Your chef says, popcorn is on the plan...One last beer?"

Jackson concurs, "You definitely need one last beer." The sound of a beer bottle opening can be heard on Jackson's end.

Shad doesn't require much prodding. He takes the beer and raises it to Benji, "OK. This is my last one until my victory beer."

Benji declares, "Never give up..."

Jackson adds, "Never surrender!"

"God, you guys are geeks."

THE JOY'S APARTMENT

The Joy is standing with her hands, palm-down on the kitchen counter. She's deep in thought...Well...The Joy's version of deep in thought. Finally, she storms over to Kimi's curtain and pulls it open. Kimi is texting. On her lap is her dinner bowl, which contains hotdogs and pasta in broth. She looks up. As if she's answering a doorbell, Kimi sings, "Who is it?"

"Oh, you know who it is."

"Hold on." Kimi sends another fast text and puts her phone aside. "OK. You have my attention."

The Joy blurts, "I had sexual relations with Vlad and it didn't help...at all!"

"Maybe you're doing it wrong."

The Joy is not amused. After a long stare, she says, "Do you have something you want to tell me?"

"You're out of hotdogs."

"You suck." The Joy leaves Kimi's corner and heads for the liquor. Kimi waits a beat and realizes that she can't and shouldn't ignore this. She carefully moves the stuff from her lap so she can get up, then grabs her bowl and follows The Joy to the kitchen.

Trying to reach out, Kimi puts an uncomfortable hand on The Joy's shoulder. "Alright, as much as I don't want to know, why was your sex session with Vlad The Impaler unsatisfying?"

The Joy slips from Kimi's touch and storms into her bedroom.

Kimi calls out, "Are you coming back?"

She quickly gets her answer when The Joy storms back with an official-looking document in her hand. The Joy slaps it down onto the counter. "Read that."

Kimi looks over and scans that letter. This is not good. She picks it up and carefully reads the entire thing. It takes a while. The Joy has nowhere to go. When she's done reading, Kimi looks at The Joy sincerely." I'm so sorry."

"Are you?"

"What does that mean?"

The Joy pours herself four fingers of whatever it was that she grabbed and drinks. Then she goes on a rant. "It means that you were a pretty mad little girl for a while there, Missy. And the whole you-should-wear-a-mask thing. And the whole you-have-too-much-sex-with-too- many-strangers thing. And the whole you-shouldn't-have-your-clients-hanging-around-the-apartment thing. And the whole, you're-taking-a-chance-with-my-life thing. Well, now you're safe. I've lost my license." Those words sink in. It's even worse now that she's said it out loud. It's like it wasn't really real until just that moment. On the edge of tears, she blurts, "Are you happy, now?"

Kimi is stunned." Do you seriously think that I turned you in? ...I guess you do." Kimi thinks, Wow, life's little up moments are just there so you have somewhere to come crashing down from. Okay. She knows what she has to do. She looks at The Joy and says, "I'll pack my things." Kimi heads to her corner.

Not what The Joy was looking for. She goes after Kimi." No, wait."

Now on her own rant, Kimi goes off. "Wait for what? You just accused me of narcing on you. I'm clearly not wanted and quite frankly, I don't want to be anywhere I'm not wanted. I haven't left this apartment since forever. But somehow, somehow, I've managed to squeeze more drama into this one little corner than I had in my entire living-outside, walking-the-earth life. I'm out." She takes the flowers off her suitcase, puts them on the La-Z-Boy and starts to pack.

The Joy breaks down, "I'm sorry."

Without looking back, "And that's supposed to be enough?"

The Joy is on the verge of tears. "Yes...for friends."

Still not turning around, Kimi says, "I'm listening."

"I'm just so upset. I need someone to blame...besides me."

Kimi stops what she's doing and turns to her friend. Crap. She's crying. Kimi gently asks, "What did you think was going to happen?"

The Joy stands there scanning her brain for an answer. All she can come up with is, "Why can't we all just get along?"

Shit. This is pathetic. "Bring it in." Kimi motions for The Joy to come get a hug."

"Really?"

"Yeah, but not too long."

They hug. From within the embrace Kimi says, "OK. That's enough."

The Joy backs up. "What am I going to do?"

Kimi hugs her again. "*We* are going to solve this."

SHAD & BENJI'S APARTMENT

It's late. Shad and Benji are passed out in the living room. Shad is stretched out on the sofa and Benji is sprawled over an armchair. There's more Benji than chair. The TV is still on and something anime is playing. Young warriors are battling giant mutants. The young warriors seem to be winning. There are bits of popcorn all over the floor along with the bottle of the "last" beer Shad was going to have before the marathon. It's laying next to all his other "last" beer bottles.

JACKSON'S APARTMENT

On Jackson's large screen TV, the same anime show is playing. He's awake, but at another screen. He's on his computer, looking through information on the legal steps one has to take to collect money for a charitable cause. Damn, this is cumbersome. He remembers why he stopped paying attention to business and legal matters. But now, it's different. It's not just academic. It's applied. He has a very clear goal and real people who he's pulled into his plan. He feels responsible for them. Jackson's going to get them across their finish line and then he's going to do the same thing for himself. He has a purpose.

STEPH'S APARTMENT/BEDROOM

Steph is putting the finishing touches on her big interview ensemble. She thinks, "Am I nervous? Hell, yeah, I am. But I can do this. Be steely." She smooths her blue blouse in the mirror. Necklace? The beaded one puts a nice pop of color by her face. But maybe that's too busy. Maybe the plain silver one. That's it. She then opens her mask drawer and scans her choices. The dark blue one matches her blouse, but is that too negative? Would something lighter be more appropriate? No. This woman's husband just died. Dark blue is perfect. Besides, it looks great with her hair.

Steph's phone rings. It's Bill. She answers, "Yeah, Bill."

"You ready?"

"I am."

Bill is all business. "Good. Now, the risk protocol is going to be tight. Mask, obviously. The van's been completely wiped down. We'll check your temperature before you get in the van and again when you get there. Davis is your camera *and* sound man. We got our special permission. You'll stand at the bottom of her front steps. Mrs. Moore will be at the top of the steps by her front door. She's going to be physically above you. That's going to feel weird. Just lock on her eyes. Davis will get it all. OK?"

Trying to match Bill's sharpness, Steph just replies, "OK."

"You're gonna be great."

Steph likes Bill. She never thought about that under Janis because Janis was always trying to knock Bill down. But he's solid. A real newsman. She asks, "Hey, how are you doing? You sound better."

"And that's why you're going to be great." With that, Bill clicks off.

Two seconds later, Steph gets a text from Jackson, "You're going to be great."

THE JOY'S APARTMENT

Kimi is setting up a watch-party for two to view Steph's big interview. This is something that would typically be The Joy's project, but The Joy is not herself and Kimi figures that this might cheer her up. She's laid out all of The Joy's favorites: s'mores-flavor Pop-Tarts, Xtra-Cheddar Flavor Blasted Goldfish, pizza-flavor egg rolls and multi-flavor cocktails with lots of rim flair. It all looks perfect. Well...you know. Kimi looks at the time and calls out, "It's almost time. I have everything ready."

No response. She tries again. "Come on. Pizza rolls...just like Mom used to make."

The Joy shuffles out of her bedroom wearing the largest, furriest, orange, cat-paw slippers of all time. The rest of her ensemble is a mix of leopard and ocelot print. And her blond hair now sports black spots.

Kimi responds to the get up, "Meow!"

The Joy mumbles, "I thought it might cheer me up."

"And?"

"Nope." The Joy plops down on the sofa, defeated. From behind all of the treats, her paw feet come up and rest on the edge of the coffee table.

JACKSON'S APARTMENT

Jackson is dressed in his expensive workout gear in the entertainment room. He saves these for special events. The large screen TV is on. Jackson does a few jumping jacks to ready himself for the news segment. Why? He's just amped up. He runs in place for a moment doing extra-high knee raises. More jumping jacks. OK. He puts his hands on the back of the sofa. He's going to watch this standing up.

He looks over his shoulder and calls out, "You should come see this."

SHAD & BENJI'S APARTMENT/SHAD'S BEDROOM

Shad is on a Zoom call with the team. Everyone is there except Christopher. Max is leading his now, regular end-of-day team call. He's being equal parts positive and critical. Positive about opportunities in the market and critical about how everyone on the team is doing. In other words, nothing new.

Shad is looking at the time. Damn, Max is running long. Max's daughter, Minnie, runs into his frame. She's about five. Max grabs her, pulls her close and finishes his thought to the team. He then turns to the child, "Minnie, tell everyone how much you're up for the year."

The child says, "Nine percent."

Sweetly, Max asks her, "Nine percent! How did you do that, sweetheart?"

Matter-of-factly, Minnie recites her line. "I followed the supply chain."

Right answer! Max hugs his prodigy one more time, then lets the child run off. "Look how smart she is. You can't beat that with a stick. Right? Right? OK kids, we'll continue this tomorrow. Follow the rubber ducks. Stay healthy. Stay wealthy."

With that, Max is gone. The rest of the team says their goodbyes and logs off. Shad pushes his chair back.

SHAD & BENJI'S APARTMENT

Benji's on the sofa with a big bowl of cauliflower. He's got Douglas with him and the TV is on. Shad scoots in and sits next to him. "Did I miss anything?"

"No. They said her story's coming up next. First they're talking about numbers still going up."

Shad asks, "The virus or the market?"

"Both."

Shad puts his hand into the bowl and shoves cauliflower in his mouth. He wasn't ready for that. "What the hell?!"

"Cauliflower."

Put out, Shad asks, "OK. Why the hell?"

"Health. You're in training. Try the dip."

Shad runs a piece of cauliflower through the dip and eats it. "Oh, my God that's good. What is that?"

Benji answers, "A blue cheese and garlic aioli."

So, not healthy."

Benji explains, "Life is balance."

THE JOY'S APARTMENT

Kimi and The Joy are on the sofa, snacking, drinking and waiting. An ad for a life insurance company is on. Kimi blurts out, "I swear. If one more person says the phrase, 'In times like these...' I'm going to stab them." Then she thinks, maybe that's not the vibe The Joy needs right now. Damn, it's so hard to stay positive.

The commercial ends and the news comes back on. The female anchor, who's dressed monochromatically but with massive, gold buttons, turns to camera. "Up next, a story that you're not going to believe. It's a tale of two heroes. One who gave the ultimate sacrifice for his country overseas, and another whose quick thinking saved a life right here on American soil. We're going to let you watch this amazing tale unfold as we saw it unfold this morning."

On the TV, Steph is standing at the front steps of a Lower East Side brownstone. A very pregnant woman of about forty stands on the top step. Well behind her, back in the hallway, are two sets of twins. Two boys and two girls. All are wearing masks. Of the group, only Steph looks well put together.

Crazy excited to see their friend in the spotlight, Kimi shoves The Joy. "That's Steph!"
"I'm aware of that."

Back on the TV, "This is Stephanie Weiss and I'm here with Mrs. Rita Moore. You may have heard about her husband, Captain John Moore, his bravery and his final letter home. Mrs. Moore, I'd first like to say how sorry we all are for your loss."
Quietly, Mrs. Moore says, "Thank you."
Steph continues, "And thank you for speaking with us. Can you tell us about that last time you spoke with John?"
Mrs. Moore answers slowly, "I talked to Johnny last Friday. He was happy. You know, to be a father again."
"Number five, right?"

"Yeah. He knew he'd never make it home in time to see the birth..." Mrs. Moore gets emotional.

With a caring and supportive smile Steph says, "But he was excited."

"Oh, yeah. Johnny loved being a dad more than anything."

"Why do you think his letter has struck such a chord with so many people?"

Mrs. Moore thinks. "I don't know. I guess, you know how people say, I wish I woulda let people know how I felt? That I loved 'em? Johnny let us know. He told us...Maybe he said it for the people who shoulda and didn't."

Just then, Rita doubles over in pain. The camera pulls back and the world can see that her water just broke. She's panicked, "Oh, no! The baby's coming! Oh, my God!"

Off camera, the voice of Davis, the camera/sound guy is saying, "Holy [BLEEP]!"

Rita is now sitting on her top step, moaning, "Help me!"

The camera keeps rolling. Steph looks around quickly, as if to see if help is coming. It's not. Then, without another obvious choice, she goes to Rita calling back to Davis, "Davis, give me your sanitizer."

The camera angle shifts sideways as Steph sanitizes her hands and up to her elbows. She then turns back to Rita. There's an iron bench on the side of the landing. Steph helps Rita onto it.

"Rita. Rita, tell me what's happening."

"The baby's coming. I can feel her."

Davis's voice is heard again calling out for a doctor. No one answers the call.

As calmly as the situation will allow, Steph asks, "Rita, I'm going to take a look. Is that OK?"

Rita bites her lip and nods her permission. As discreetly as possible, Steph looks under Rita's dress. Any improprieties are blocked from view by the back of Steph's shoulders. She turns to camera and shakes her head to Davis. There's a grave look on her face. She turns back to Rita and in a clear, even tone says, "Rita, you're right. I can see her."

Rita cries, "Oh, my God!"

Back in their apartment, Kimi and The Joy are clutching hands. Kimi cries, "Oh, my God!"

Back on TV Steph says to Rita, "Rita, listen to me. Are you listening?" Rita nods. "Your baby is breach. I see her feet."

Frightened, all Rita can get out is," No."

"It's going to be OK." Steph reassures her. "Your baby's feet are beautiful, Rita." With that, Rita calms down a bit and almost smiles.

Steph calls out to Rita's children, "Kids, I need someone to boil water and someone to get some clean towels." The children in the hall scatter.

Steph turns back to Rita, "See. We already have help. OK, now, I need you to scoot forward. Can you do that?" Rita nods and scoots forward.

Davis calls for help again.

Steph explains, "We're going to let this little girl do most of the work. Here's what's going to happen. First, when I tell you, you're gonna push. Then when I tell you, you're gonna stop, even though you'll want to keep pushing. You got that? It's really important that you stop when I say stop. Promise?"

"I promise."

Steph gets into position and says, "Let's do this. Rita, give me one good hard push until I say stop. Ready?"

"Ready."

"Now—push!"

Rita bears down and pushes hard without making a sound. She's the picture of silent strength. Steph holds up a hand. "Stop!"

Rita does as told. Steph exclaims, "Oh, my God! Rita, that was amazing. Holy…! She's mostly out! Look how clever you are. It's just the head now. This is the hard part. We're going to let her hang out for a moment and the weight of her own head is going to help her out."

Steph checks her watch. One of Rita's kids returns with a towel. Steph takes it. Rita starts making faces. "Can I push?"

"Not yet."

It's clearly getting harder for Rita by the second." Now?"

"Hold on, kiddo."

"I really need to push."

"You will."

Rita can't take much more. "When?"

Steph readies herself, "…Now! Push!"

Rita gives a good, strong push and a moment later Steph is holding a baby. The river of emotions that washes over each of their faces is the best television of the year. Off-camera Davis says, "Holy [BLEEP]! We're getting an EMMY!"

Sweetly, Steph tells Rita, "You made a baby." She hands the little girl, wrapped in a towel, to her mother.

Cradling the newborn, Rita greets the baby girl, "Hello, Jonny."

Steph looks back at Davis and the camera. In a bit of a daze, "Are you still rolling?"

The news then cuts back to the anchor who is noticeably moved by the footage. "And that's how it happened this morning on the front steps of the Moore home. We thank our fast-thinking reporter, Stephanie Weiss, and are happy to report that a doctor is now with Mrs. Moore and little baby, Jonny. Everyone is home and doing well. More after this commercial break."

A commercial for baby food comes on the TV. Kimi and The Joy sit on the sofa, completely stunned. Their drinks are empty and they are motionless. Without moving a muscle, Kimi says, "What the fuck just happened?"

JACKSON'S APARTMENT

Alone, Jackson stands up straight with a tear in his eye and gives a strong, slow, proud round of applause.

SHAD & BENJI'S APARTMENT

Benji is jumping up and down. Shad is pumping his fists, not knowing what else to do with himself. Douglas is confused and barking. The thrill was nothing that either of them was prepared for.

Benji shouts, "That was the coolest thing, ever!"

Incredulously, Shad says, "She delivered a baby."

"I know!"

"On TV."

"I know!"

"Our friend is the coolest person, ever."

They high-five each other, then realize the moment calls for more. They chest butt.

STEPH'S APARTMENT/BEDROOM

Steph is sitting cross-legged on her bed. She's been home from the shoot for some time, has showered…twice, and is wearing a tank top and sweatshorts. She's drinking from a bottle of wine. No need for a glass. The TV and the light from her bathroom are the only lights in the room. She can feel her heart beating fast. It had slowed down, but watching the events of the morning unfold before her got it going again. She thinks, "This morning I delivered a baby. It actually happened. I know, because I just saw it. Holy shit. How did I stay so calm? Was I calm? No. It was like time slowed down and I was an actor from the midwife show."

Then a new, unpleasant thought hits her. "Can I be sued? I broke protocol."

Then, an even less pleasant thought hits her. "What if something had gone wrong?" She starts spinning scenarios in her head where things go sideways and the baby doesn't make it. Awful versions of the morning that ends with her losing everything. She could be in jail. "Why did I do that? I'm a fucking idiot!" She can feel herself starting to shake and takes another sip of wine.

Steph feels her phone vibrate, again. She can see that she has a ton of unanswered messages. She doesn't want to talk to anyone. Not yet. It's Jackson. No. Her head is swimming.

Almost on top of Jackson's text vibration, her phone rings. It's Bill. Fuck. She knows she has to take this. She lets it ring as many times as she dares. The longer she waits, the more her life gets to be that part before she gets fired…or worse.

She steadies her nerves.

"Yeah, Bill."

JACKSON'S APARTMENT

Jackson's at his computer, but looking at his phone. Nothing. He turns back to his computer. He's on a site for someone's annual, charity marathon event. He's looking at all the legalese for terms and conditions and trying to borrow it for his own legalese. But he's distracted. Everything is getting so serious. This is exactly what he'd gotten good at avoiding. He can't focus.

Jackson gets up and goes to part of his in-home obstacle course. He grabs the pole from the salmon ladder and starts working his way up.

THE JOY'S APARTMENT

Kimi and The Joy are on the sofa in the exact same spot they were in when they watched the local news. The national news has started. Steph's story has been picked up there, too. Kimi is looking at her phone and sees Steph's story in the Google headline news. Her phone vibrates in her hand. It's a text from Steph that reads, "Zoom?"

STEPH'S APARTMENT/BEDROOM

Steph's on her bed, now with her computer on her lap. She's cradling her bottle of wine like a child and clicks to start her video call. When she joins the call, The Joy and Kimi are already there.

Kimi has her hands on her head. "What the hell took you so long?"

"Nice to see you, too."

The Joy is kinder, "Wait. Hold on, lady." She and Kimi stand up and applaud.

Steph bows her head in appreciation. "Thanks, you guys."

After they sit back down, Kimi says, "You...are a fucking rockstar. I mean, you were so cool. And you looked fucking amazing. You stayed beautiful the entire time."

The Joy adds, "And you're a baby birther."

Steph: "Well."

Kimi asks, "You just knew how to do that?"

"I told you I binged *Call The Midwife*. I just...I don't know. I was like, all of a sudden I was in the show. Like, literally, in it. Everything else in the world dropped away, time slowed down and I was in lockstep with this woman I'd never met. Seriously."

Bummed, The Joy says, "She didn't name the baby after you. That would have been a nice gesture."

"Well, she named her after her dead husband. I figure I'll give her a pass."

The Joy sighs, "Still..."

Kimi lifts her glass. "Name or not, cheers to our friend Steph who saved the goddamn day." They all cheer and drink. Then there's silence. Kimi breaks it. "Come on. Spill it. Tell us about it."

The Joy agrees, "Yeah. We want to hear everything...Like, what's going on with you and Jackson?"

Kimi shoves The Joy. "No. We want to hear about how you helped someone give fucking birth on fucking television...then the Jackson thing."

"Seriously, it's a blur. I just reacted. I didn't even know I was being filmed. Then after the baby was born, I don't remember how long, this doctor shows up and moves Rita into the building. I was just standing there covered in blood. I think my blouse is ruined...I loved that blouse...Davis, the camera guy, he's squirting hand sanitizer all over me. After a while, he drives me home, I put all my clothes in a corner, and stand in the shower for about an hour. There were so many thoughts running through my head and I couldn't focus on one of them...Oh, my God...Wait 'til Janis sees it. She's gonna shit."

Kimi laughs, "I'm sure she's seen it. It's everywhere."

Thinking about that, then feeling the weight of it, Steph slowly says, "Yeah." After a long silence, she adds, "Let's talk about something else."

The Joy: "Let's not."

Kimi: "Yeah, come on. You're getting a big raise, right? You know, we're gonna totally sponge off you the second we get released."

"No big raise."

Kimi's putout for her friend. "What? That's bullshit. You're like a news woman with super powers. Oh, you're getting a raise."

"It's not that simple. I broke protocols. I wasn't supposed to get near Mrs. Moore, let alone deliver her damn baby. I have zero medical background. I way overstepped. Like, in the world of overstepping, I just ran an ultra. So many things could have gone so wrong. Legal is all over it. The station could get sued. The network could get sued. Bill's going to bat for me, but...who knows. I don't know. He said to sit tight and he'd let me know. Fuck. Of all the scenarios I've ever run in my head about my career path, this was never one of them. I really thought I'd prepped myself for every possibility. You know, what would I do if an anchor got sick and I was suddenly called up to take over. Or, what if I covered a small story and one of the high-ups fell in love with me and had to have me for the Washington desk...or the national nightly news. I know what I'd wear, how I'd accessorize..."

Kimi: "So wait. When you play out possible scenarios of how your life could turn out, they're all positive?"

"Sure. Mostly. Sometimes I get all Ida and think about what I'd do if I get a last-minute assignment and all my blouses were wrinkled and that somehow led to ending up at the bottom of a stairwell with my head cracked open."

Kimi: "And that is why you are you."

Ignoring that, or not even hearing it, Steph says, "*And*...Until we hear from legal, I'm not supposed to be talking to anyone about this. My cell hasn't stopped. Texts, calls. It's crazy."

Not very convincingly, The Joy says, "Listen, lady, I bet it will all work out."

Kimi turns to The Joy, "Wow. Remind me not to hire you for a pep talk."

Happy to have the focus off of her for a moment, Steph asks the Joy, "What's up? You don't seem like you."

Kimi: "The Joy lost her license."

"What? Why?"

Kimi gets up. From out of the video frame she calls back to The Joy, "You explain it. I'll refresh our medicine."

"Well, apparently, someone turned me in for seeing clients in an..." she makes air quotes for key words, "*unsafe* environment when I was supposed to be closed for quarantine. Apparently, I'm not an *essential* business."

Steph: "You are to me."

"See. That's what I thought. Ask any of my clients. They'll tell you how essential I am. Well, all of them except the one who turned me in."

Kimi returns with new drinks, "We all think you're essential."

Steph: "I'll cheers to that."

The Joy starts to feel slightly emboldened by the support of her friends mixed with equal parts liquid courage. She raises her glass. "Cheers to me!"

In unison, Kimi and Steph say, "Cheers to you."

The Joy has a revelation, "Oh, I think I'm going to change my name to, The *Essential* Joy...Hey, I like that."

Kimi: "Only if the 'Essential' is silent."

Steph: "So, what are you going to do?"

"Fuck if I know." She turns to Kimi. "I think you're rubbing off on me."

"Well, here's a topic changer. I have sold, to date, wait...drum roll..." Kimi grabs her phone and quickly checks on her masks stats. It doesn't take long as it's pretty much the only web page she looks at any more. The info comes up. "Oh, shit."

Steph: "What?"

" I've sold eight hundred masks. Exactly eight hundred. Do you know how crazy lucky that is?"

Steph: "It's not luck. It's hard work."

"No. I mean it's a lucky number. Well, now it's eight hundred and one, but fuck that. Eight hundred is so lucky in the Chinese culture. I'd tell my mother if I didn't think I'd get a lecture about being her disappointing first-gen child."

"My roommate the mask mogul. To girl power!"

Abruptly, Kimi declares, "No. Fuck girl power. Girl power is crap. It's just a phrase to patronize women. You never hear, 'boy power.' You know why? Because they have fucking power and they know it. They don't have to say it. And they wouldn't say 'boy power.' They'd say, 'man power.' I want straight-up, full-blown *power* power. For all of us."

The Joy is stirred up by Kimi's mini-speech, "Fuck, yeah!"

And Steph makes three. "Fuck, yeah."

Kimi: "Crazy times...Hey, how 'bout that Jackson?"

Steph: "Oh, I have to go."

The Joy: "No you don't."

Looking at her phone, Steph says, "Actually, I do. Bill's calling. Love you both."

Kimi and The Joy can see Steph answering her phone but can't hear the conversation. They try to read Steph's body language, then Steph's screen goes black.

JACKSON'S APARTMENT

Jackson is back at his computer, sweaty with the dowel from the salmon ladder leaning on his desk. He's putting the finishing touches on a website he's titled, the *We Are One - Marathon In Place.* He feels that for no background in this kind of thing, he did OK. It's easy to navigate and that's the important thing. He clicks the publish button. Jackson sits back, puts his feet on the desk, grabs a bag of salty snacks from the floor next to him and admires his work. He feels OK about himself.

Still no messages on his phone. Maybe he needs to train some more.

ZOOM MASTERS

STEPH'S APARTMENT

Steph's apartment feels empty. With no lights on, there's still plenty of light from outside. It's quiet. An alarm goes off in her bedroom. Moments later, Steph scoots in still covered in sleep. In her tank top and men's silk pajama bottoms she heads to her computer. She opens it and realizes she's empty-handed. She thinks, do I really need a drink? Then thinks, it's not need, it's habit. Let's stick with the familiar. She goes and pulls an opened bottle of white wine from the fridge, grabs a glass from the sink and goes back to her computer. Once she's all set up, she runs her fingers through her hair. Hmm. She gets back up and shakes her head upside down to give herself the appropriate amount of volume. Back in place. She takes a sip of wine, opens her eyes extra wide, in an attempt to look awake and clicks onto the video call.

Everyone is already there. In unison, they all cheer and spin groggers, tin clackety noisemakers that create a hell of a racket. Completely touched, Steph is speechless for a moment. "Thank you, guys."

The Joy tees them up, "Two, three, four…"

As Shad starts singing, the rest clap a beat. Shad sings Donna Summer, "Ahhhh, Love to love you, BABY. Ahhh, love to love you BABY…"

Next, The Joy sings Britney Spears, "Hit me BABY one more time…"

Up next is Kimi who does Vanilla Ice, "Ice, ice BABY. Da nah nah nah nah nah nah nah, ice, ice BABY…"

Then Jackson sings the Smash Mouth tune, "Can't get enough of you, BABY…"

Then Benji does Whitney Houston with a shocking amount of skill and a beautiful tone, "Whatever you want from me. I'm givin' you everything, I'm your BABY tonight…"

Then they all join in for the Ronettes', "Be my, be my little BABY. Be my BABY now. Woe, woe, woe, woe, woe!"

Steph is gob-smacked, "Oh-my-God. Seriously? That was so amazing. Seriously. Wow. Just, wow."

They all over-talk their, "Your welcomes."

The Joy points out, "It would have been better, but you're quite late."

"Yeah. Sorry. I was sleeping. This whole thing really knocked me out. I slept most of the day. I just woke up."

Kimi: "God, I hate you."

With love, Steph says, "I hate you too, girlfriend."

The Joy: "So what did they say at work? Are you going to the slammer?"

Shad: "Wait. Are you in trouble?"

With a slight laugh, Steph says, "No. Kimi, you were right. Everyone has seen this thing. It's totally viral. And since, at least so far, Mrs. Moore and the baby seem happy and healthy, and not litigious, I still have a job. In fact, get this, I'm going to be interviewed on *Morning In America*."

Shad: "Holy shit!"

"Yeah. First the plan was for me to lay way low. Wait and see...and hope and pray. But the 'Morning News Show' thinks they'll pull big numbers if they get me up fast. You know, before the next national shit show."

The Joy: "Tomorrow? I'll watch."

Benji: "I'm so proud of you."

"You and my folks. Oh, my God, Ida can't stop kvelling. I swear, I've given her bragging power for years. It's like the best pre-Mother's Day gift of all time."

Shad thinks. "I totally forgot about Mother's Day."

The revelation starts hitting all of them. Kimi moans, "Oh, shit. Mother's Day."

The Joy: "I bet your, *oh shit*, will be better than my *oh shit*."

"Did you mom suddenly turn Chinese?"

Jackson: "I've got my call scheduled. They're eight hours ahead in the UAE. I'm getting up at 3 a.m. to be on with Mommy at eleven her time."

The Joy: "*Mommy*. That's so cute."

Jackson: "I'm a very cute guy."

The Joy: "Nudge, nudge. Wink, wink."

Shad: "Who are you talking too?"

The Joy: "Oh, yeah. We're not alone. Sorry."

Benji: "I wish I could go and actually see my parents...They only have me...I bet my mom's going to be sad."

Steph: "When Ida told me not to come, I almost lost it...Let's move on to something happy."

The Joy: "OK, who doesn't know that I lost my license?"

Benji: "I lost my license a couple of times. Remember in high school when I drove into the mascot? It *was* an accident...but I did really hate that guy."

Kimi: "No. She lost her hair stylist's license."

Shad: "That sucks."

The Joy: "It sucks so much."

After a long silence filled with no one knowing what to say to console The Joy, Steph offers, "So let's try again. Something happy...Go!"

Shad: "Did we tell you all about the marathon?"

Kimi: "You're running a marathon in your apartment. You're a freak. Yes, we know."

Shad: "Nooo. It's so much better. Jackson, you tell the ladies."

Jackson: "Thank you, Shad. Ladies, our Shad is not running *a* marathon. He's running in *the*... *All For One, Marathon In Place*. A virtual event to raise money for out-of-work restaurant workers."

Benji: "That last part was my idea."

Jackson: "Yes. It will be held on May 26th and we already have people signing up."

Kimi: "You actually found more freaks willing to run an entire marathon in their apartment?"

Jackson: "Yes."

Steph: "That's fantastic. What a great story."

Shad: "Want to cover it?"

Steph: "What? No. I can't."

Shad: "Why not. You're the new media darling. You can do whatever you want."

Steph: "First, I can't do whatever I want. No one can. And second, I take assignments...when I get them. I don't come up with stories."

Shad: "You're not coming up with a story. You're covering a feel-good piece. Aren't you the local news' feel-good gal now?"

The Joy: "Nudge, nudge. Wink, wink...And yes, I know you all can hear me."

Jackson: "It would be a great story. Let's say we get a few hundred people to do it. You follow, let's say, ten of them on their run—all shot by someone in their home with a hand-held device. It's all very safe. Everyone is missing watching sports right now..."

Kimi: "I'm not."

Jackson is undeterred. "Plus, you keep a running tally of how much we're raising. You throw in a few sad stories of restaurant workers... It's a news story, a sporting event and a fundraiser. It's a triple threat with a bow on it." Everyone is so utterly thrown by Jackson's competence that they just sit and drink.

Shad: "Just say that you'll think about it."

Steph: "I'll think about it. But first, I need Benji to sing to me again."

Benji: "If we get the story, you get the song."

Steph: "Fair enough...Listen guys. I'm pretty spent. I'm gonna go."

The Joy: "You can't. We haven't shared out secrets yet."

Steph: "I'll share a secret next time. I promise."

The Joy: "OK. But we can't put if off any longer or we'll be in danger of spilling everything to each other in our regular conversation. And what fun is that?"

Steph: "Promise. And thank you all for the songs."

Shad: "Thank you for saving a life."

Steph looks truly touched at that and signs off. She gets up and walks to her window wall. With her wine glass in hand, she looks over the city. It's so quiet from where she's standing.

MOTHER'S DAY

JACKSON'S APARTMENT/BEDROOM

It's almost 3 o'clock in the morning. Jackson is in only boxer shorts, stretched out on top of the huge, fluffy comforter on his parents' bed. It's so thick that he's sunk down into it. Even in the dark, his brown skin is in contrast with the lush bedding. The alarm in his Apple Watch goes off. Without moving, he easily opens his eyes. After a moment, he hits off the alarm. At peace with himself like few people ever get to be, Jackson sits up, then reaches for a remote. He hits a button that gently brings up the lighting. He looks around and smiles to himself, happy just thinking about his mother.

After a quick visit to the bathroom to take care of business, he runs a brush through his hair, puts on a nice white shirt, props up some pillows, and gets back on the bed. He picks up his phone and clicks on his mother's picture.

After just a few rings, the voice he's been waiting for answers, "Is this my Jacky?"

"Yes Mommy, it's me. Mommy, tap the video button."

There she is. Jackson's mother is beaming at him from the phone. For a moment, they take each other in. Mrs. Asghar is on her balcony, sitting in a cream-colored chair with navy pillows and gold piping. Her white clothing with colorful accents is blowing in the light breeze. Her hair doesn't move.

"Happy Mother's Day."

"You made your mother so happy."

"Good. That's my job. So what do you have planned to do today?"

"I plan to miss my children, but that's a mother's job...So many places are closed here. But Daddy is surprising me with a lovely lunch from Byblos Sur Mer and a new bracelet."

"How do you know that if he's surprising you?"

"Your father can never keep a secret...I've already heard from all of your sisters...and my beautiful grandchildren...I look forward to the day when I'll get a Mother's Day call from your children. Or better, when I can hold them in my arms and sing to them like I used to sing to you. Do you remember?"

"I remember."

"You're a bad boy for making me wait."

"I know, Mommy."

"And Ruby...What are we going to do about your sister? She could be so pretty if she only tried. You know, Mrs. Hadi's oldest son would be a perfect match for her...He's awkward as well. But he no longer wears braces and his teeth are very straight. He's already working with his father and someday the funeral home will be his. Mrs. Hadi said that he would be willing to start corresponding with Ruby. I think you should talk to your sister. Tell her how good this will be for her."

"Mommy, I don't want to get involved."

Without losing any of the kindness in her voice, but suddenly firm, Mrs. Asghar says, "But you will for me, won't you? As a Mother's Day gift."

Jackson does his best to not let his reluctance show on his face. "...Of course I will."

"You're a good boy. Now, your father would like to speak with you." Mrs. Asghar looks somewhere off-screen and calls to her husband. "Malika, come talk to Jacky."

Jackson waits for his father to join the call. He wonders what not-so-subtle nudge his father will give to get him to go back to school? Should he share his thoughts and plans with his father? No. Mr. Asghar leans into the frame. Mrs. Asghar whispers to her husband, "Work on him, but not too hard."

Mr. Asghar says, "There is my boy."

"Hello father."

"Are you still in bed?"

"It's three o'clock in the morning here, Father."

"So it is. So it is. And what are you going to do with your day, now that you're awake?"

"I'm helping a friend with a project."

"Would you like to tell me about it?"

"It's charity work. I'll tell you more about it as it comes together."

"Charity work. Good for you, Jacky! I'm very happy to hear this, son. It's important to do good works. Does this mean that perhaps you're ready to take your life seriously and finish school?"

"I'm thinking about a lot of things right now. I'll let you know when it comes together."

"You have a fine mind, son. But you can't win with the horse in the barn. Do you understand me?"

With that, Mrs. Asghar gives her husband a shove and whispers to him, "Too much."

Jackson says, "I understand, Father."

"Good boy. Well, wish your mother a happy Mother's Day. I have a few big surprises for her." Mrs. Asghar shares a knowing wink with her son and smiles.

"Happy Mother's Day, Mommy. I love you."

"I love you too, Jacky. And don't forget your promise. Talk to Ruby."

"Yes, Mommy."

Jackson clicks off the call and falls back on the bed. He thinks, "God, this bed feels good. How long can I go without moving?"

SHAD'S & BENJI'S APARTMENT

Shad's holding his cell phone while leaning into the fridge. He scans the shelves for an unhealthy snack while he listens to his mother's line ring.

Mr. Perkins answers. "Yeah?"

Shad stands up straight. "Dad?"

"Were you expecting someone else?"

"No. I guess I was thinking about Mom and...doesn't matter. How are you?" Shad grabs a chocolate milk and walks the apartment as his father talks.

"We're fine. Bored, like everyone else, but fine."

"Good." There's a long pause as neither knows what to say to the other. Shad doesn't question that his father loves him. He does wonder why this is always so damn hard.

"I suppose you want to talk to your mother."

"Yeah. That would be great."

Suddenly excited, Mr. Perkins says, "Oh, did you hear what Joe did?"

"No. I haven't heard anything."

"So you know that all the school sports are on hold right now. Well, not football! Not at your brother's school. Joe is doing virtual football practice for his kids."

"It's not football season."

"Exactly. And your brother had the smart idea to get these kids up and moving, and having a positive sports experience right now. Drills, strategy, strength training, all of it. It's great."

"Wow. That does sound great...Hey, speaking of that, I almost forgot. I'm going to be running a marathon."

A marathon? Outside?"

"No. In my apartment."

"That's just crazy. Hold on, I'll get your mother." Mr. Perkins calls out for Shad's mother to pick up the phone. Shad wonders why he tries. And why does it matter?

"Here's your mother."

"Thanks d..."

But dad's gone. Mrs. Perkins picks up, "Hey, baby."

"Hey, Mom. Happy Mother's Day."

"Thank you, sweetie. Oh, before I forget, I got the pears. Oh, they're so good. So sweet. You *and* the pears. Thank you, baby."

Shad settles comfortably on the sofa. Douglas joins him. "You're very welcome. Tell me how you're doing."

"Well, let's see. With the office closed, I'm just spending my time being a fool. That's all. I'm trying, once again to get those darn tomatoes going. You'd think I'd learn. I'm just a cockeyed optimist."

"There are worse things to be. What else is going on?"

"Chad and Shanna and the kids are coming over for dinner. Your brother's going to try to wrestle the grill from your father. Should be interesting...and loud, but nice. Now, you tell me about you. How are things going on in the world of high-finance?"

"Pretty good, all things considered. If we keep our clients connected and calm, and get them to just watch the numbers go back up, I think we'll be OK."

"I'm sure you'll be even better then OK."

Shad wonders if he should try his other piece of news again. Why not? "So I was telling Dad, I'm going to be running a marathon."

"You're kidding. When?"

"On the twentieth-sixth."

"Of this month?"

"That's right."

"Oh, baby, I don't know that you should be outside for that long."

"No, Mom. I'm going to run the whole thing in my apartment."

After a long pause, Mrs. Perkins says, with love and a bit of a laugh in her voice, "My men are so crazy."

"It's a charity run. We're getting a ton of people to participate. We started just thinking about New York, but now we have people all over the country. Everyone'll run in their own home and all the money we raise goes to support people in the restaurant industry."

"Isn't that something. Well, you are certainly giving me quite the Mother's Day present. Oh, baby, I'm so proud of you. I think you get that sweet side from me."

"I know I do."

Suddenly distracted, Mrs. Perkins says, "Well, I better go. Chad just drove up and I can already hear him arguing with your father."

"OK, Mom. Happy Mother's Day."

"Thank you, baby. You be careful running around that apartment. Tell the big roommate of yours to keep his enormous feet out of your way."

"Done." Shad hangs up. He thinks about how his mom always knew how to make him feel good. Then he thinks about the last time he watched his father and brother fight over the best way to grill a steak. He's happy to be right where he is.

THE JOY'S APARTMENT/BEDROOM

The Joy is killing time by draping different scarves over her bedside lamp. She lays a scarf on and assesses the color it sends to her walls. Hmm. No. She tries another. That one isn't making her happy, either. When she picks up the next scarf, she uncovers her phone. She stares at it for a while and thinks, "I should just call and get it over with. God, this is going to suck." Then she thinks, No, if she waits till later, there's a good chance Betty will be at the club. "Leave a message. That's the safest thing." She ignores the phone and goes back to the scarfs.

STEPH'S APARTMENT

Steph finishes a workout and sits on her Peloton for a moment. She checks her stats while catching her breath. Not bad. Completely respectable. After a few minutes, she gets off and brings her water bottle over to her computer to check work email. A few messages, but nothing seems like it's screaming for her attention. Not long after playing midwife, the station started playing gatekeeper with anything related to the event. For now, she's happy about that. But then...shit. An email from Janis to her personal account. This is the perfect time to call Ida. She picks up her phone and hits the appropriate speed-dial.

A moment later, Ida bursts onto the phone, "I'm talking to Mrs. Morning News Show?"

"Nope. Just your daughter."

"Stephanie Cronkite."

"Yes. I've changed my last name to Cronkite. You guys don't mind, right?"

"As long as you have that face, everyone will know that you're ours."

"I'm yours. Happy Mother's Day, Mom."

Ida is still busting, "Happy Mother's Year. The entire neighborhood is congratulating us for having such an amazing, beautiful daughter. Your father and I are so proud."

"Thanks, Mom."

"I'm just so sorry about the blouse."

"Yeah, well, casualty of war."

"Wait, I'm gonna put you on speaker. Your father has something to say to you." A moment later, the line goes dead. Steph just shakes her head. While she waits, she looks at her inbox again. The mail from Janis is just sitting there, staring at her.

Her phone rings. Steph answers, "Yeah, Ma."

"What just happened?"

"I'm guessing you disconnected us when you tried to switch to speaker."

Oh. Should I try again?"

With the abandon of a high-roller, Steph says, "Why not. Let's live on the edge."

"Like Thelma and Louise... Hold on. Here we go."

Steph thinks, "Over the cliff."

Suddenly louder, Ida calls out, "Can you hear us?"

"I hear *you.*"

Mur chimes in, "I'm here."

"Hey, dad."

He says, "Steph, are you ready for this?"

"Ready."

"You remember Pageant's on Ventnor?"

"Sure."

"I go to the gym with Gus. You met Gus. He told me today that they're naming a hoagie after you."

"Please don't tell me what's on it."

"Pastrami, coleslaw, Russian dressing. It's really just a Jewish sandwich in a hoagie. Pastrami, coleslaw, Russian dressing. That's a Jewish sandwich. Anyway, we're all really proud of you. Really proud, girl."

"Thanks, Dad...And tell Gus I said..."

With zero emotion, Ida tells her, "He's gone."

"What?"

"You know your father's not a phone talker. But he's very proud. We're all just kvelling. I know now that I never really knew what kvelling was before. It's like experiencing your first real orgasm."

Steph winces. "Oh, Mom! No."

"It's fine. It was with your father."

"That's great."

"You should be glad the sex with him is so good. It took us a long time to have you. Years. Thank God we enjoyed the trying."

In sarcastic agreement, Steph says, "Thank God." She wonders if she's the only person who has these conversations with their mother.

"So now that you're so successful, do you think you could slow down long enough to find the love of your life? Or maybe even a date?"

"I'm kind of seeing someone."

"And?"

"And nothing. It's new. He's nice. We'll see."

"Can I at least ask if he's Jewish?"

"No. You can't ask."

"You're killing me. You know that?"

Steph lovingly changes the topic saying, "Happy Mother's Day, Mom."

"I get it...I thank you for the phone call, and the Mother's Day wishes, and the card, and being our beautiful, thoughtful daughter. I love you very much."

"I love you too, Mom. Talk to you tomorrow."

"OK, tomorrow. I love you. Goodbye."

Steph hangs up and wonders why she said anything about seeing someone. How much does she like him? He's so damn hot. And there's more there than she originally thought. And he comes from money, so that would never be a concern. And he's so damn hot. And sooo, not Jewish. She sits for a while thinking, then Janis's email catches her eye again.

THE JOY'S APARTMENT/FIRE ESCAPE

Kimi is on the fire escape, one of her three usual spots. How many places are there to go, really? She's on her cell with Milli. Kimi asks, "Did you talk to Mom yet?"

"First thing. Early and over."

"You're so brave."

"You'll be fine. Just do it."

"Maybe I'll tell her I'm becoming a heterosexual doctor."

"Can you do that?"

"Pretty sure, no."

"Hey, speaking of doctors, everyone here loves your masks. They're all wearing them. I mean, not at work, but it's kind of their casual-wear."

"That's cool."

"How are sales?"

"Surprisingly OK. If it keeps up, I'll be able to pay you back pretty soon."

"You don't have to..."

Kimi cuts her off, "I'm paying you back."

"Good. I'd hate to think I have a freeloader for a sister."

"So harsh."

"Just call Mom and get it over with. You're only making it worse. Hey, you're a not-quite-successful business woman now. Tell her that."

"I'm so glad I called you."

"You so are. Call Mom."

"I will."

"Call. Now. I'm hanging. Call. Text me if you need to. Call. Goodbye."

Milli hangs up. Kimi wonders what she'd do without her. No need. She has her. She stares at her phone for a long while. A voice from above snaps her out of her private world. She looks up and sees Balcony Mom, holding her baby, looking down at her.

Balcony Mom calls down, "Just call your mother already."

Looking up Kimi calls back, "Mind your own business, Stella."

"Call."

"Hey, Stella…" Kimi thinks, Great, now I'm a cliché. "…Fine. I'm calling." Kimi thinks about how much she has enjoyed her courtyard people. She adds, "Happy Mother's Day."

"Thanks…Call."

Kimi turns her attention back to her phone. After one last beat, she rips off the Band-Aid. While the phone rings, she wonders what the smart approach should be. Fuck. Should have thought this out before.

Mrs. Chu answers as if she doesn't have caller ID, "Hello?"

"Hey, Mom. It's Kimi."

Mrs. Chu speaks with an accent, but slowly enough to do her best to pronounce everything correctly, "Hello Kimi. My last child to call today. Put me on video. I have paper children. I want to see you."

Kimi knows that video will only give her mother more things to pick at, but she's trapped. Paper children means her mother wants more than framed pictures to look at. She clicks on the video. There's her mother. Mrs. Chu is a small, tidy looking lady bundled in a very big knit sweater. Her smile says she's deciding if she likes what she sees. "I see you now."

"I see you, too. You look cold, Mom. Tell Dad to turn the heat up."

"And waste all that money? That what sweaters are for."

Why fight it? Kimi just says, "Yup…I called to wish you a happy Mother's Day."

"OK. I'm waiting. Make me a wish."

Slowly, almost as if to a child, "I wish you a happy Mother's Day."

"Oh, thank you." As Mrs. Chu talks, she walks around her home. Nothing flashy, but immaculate. "You want say hello to your brother, Chin?"

"That's OK."

Mrs. Chu opens a door without knocking. Kimi can hear her brother. Chin calls out, "Hey! Mom. I'm getting changed." Mrs. Chu turns the phone and Kimi sees her brother scramble to get his slacks up. He looks over and with resign, "Hi Kimi."

With the same resign Kimi echoes her brother, "Hi, Chin."

With that, Mrs. Chu turns the phone back on herself and walks to the kitchen. "Where are you? Is that a ladder?"

"I'm on the fire escape. It's like a little balcony."

"You should clean it. It look messy."

"OK, Mom. I'll clean the fire escape."

"Milli said to me you don't sell flowers now. You need to go back to school. Or find a good husband with a good job."

Kimi knows better than to go down this road, but... "Did Milli tell you I started a new business?"

"You can't start a business. You need a business degree for that."

"Well, I guess you don't. Because I did it. And I'm making money."

"How much?"

"It's a new business, Mom. Nothing big yet."

"Always *yet*."

"I'm selling face masks with floral designs." Kimi knows to not mention the smart-ass sayings. This time she listens to her better judgment. She adds, "Milli's co-workers have been buying them. And I'm starting to pick up traction online."

Mrs. Chu processes this, "That good. That good...I still say you better off finding a good man. What happen when your business fail? You want to be homeless? You know the Wongs from over next to King's Highway? Their daughter Lili just got married to a very nice dentist. Very good business."

"I will definitely think about that."

"Good. Good. But don't think too much."

"Why? Are we in danger of running out of eligible dentists?"

"You laugh. But it a numbers game."

Enough of this. Kimi can't imagine ever coming clean to her folks about being gay, but that doesn't make pretending any less hurtful. She tries to not let herself think about what it might be like to share a holiday with her family and a welcomed partner. She's at her limit. Planning her exit, Kimi says, "Well, Mom..."

"I know what, *Well mom* means. Hold on. You need to see this." As Mrs. Chu walks to the living room, she calls out, "Chin, come hold my phone."

Mr. Chu, dressed in a white shirt, slacks and slippers, is sitting on the slip-covered sofa watching the news. Mrs. Chu says to him, "Get up. Get up. I'm talking to Kimi. She wants to see our TikTok Dance." Mr. Chu rises to his feet without saying a word. He's clearly been through this routine before. Chin comes into view and Kimi watches the world temporarily go on its side as the phone gets handed off.

Mr. and Mrs. Chu are now standing next to each other. Mr. Chu is still watching the news. Mrs. Chu says, "Ready...go." She and her husband launch into matching dance moves with no music. Kimi shakes her head trying to decide if this is crazy or if she loves it? The conclusion: C) A and B are correct. Oh, my God. When the routine is over, Mr. Chu sits right back down in front of the news. Chin turns the phone on himself and whispers, "They've been working on that for weeks."

The phone is handed back to Mrs. Chu. She's breathless, "How about that?"

Kimi is sincerely enthusiastic, "That was great. I'd clap if I wasn't holding the phone."

Quietly, Mrs. Chu says, "I think I'm more on fleek than you're father."

"You are totally fly."

"You could TikTok me a dance."

"I'm nowhere near as on fleek as you guys."

"You can always try."

Kimi thinks that that was almost fun, but there's likely nothing else good or safe to say. So she again says, "Well mom..."

"I know, *well, Mom*. OK. OK. You think about what I told you."

"I will."

"Give me my wish one more time."

It takes Kimi a moment to figure out what her mother is asking for. Once she solves the puzzle, "I wish you a happy Mother's Day."

"Thank you."

Kimi hangs up the call and sits there for a moment thinking about everything she didn't say, before she realizes that the voice coming down from above is for her.

Playfully, Balcony Woman calls out, "Was that so hard?"

"Yes. Yes it was."

THE JOY'S APARTMENT

Kimi is deftly making her way back in over the windowsill juju when The Joy walks through the room towards the kitchen with her head down. Kimi says, "Your turn."

"What?"

"I called home. Your turn."

The Joy shutters, then assesses the meaning. "Wow. Did you see that? That can't be a good sign."

"The longer you put it off..." Kimi leaves the thought open-ended. She goes to the fridge, grabs a can of wine and heads to her corner. Without looking back she says, "I'll join for a drink when it's over." With that, her curtains close behind her.

The Joy calls back, "You shouldn't drink canned wine. There are chemicals." No response. The Joy thinks, "Not yet. Maybe there's something good on TV." She goes to the sofa and places herself in the corner. What's on? House hunting show...no. Cooking show...no. Another cooking show...no. Renovation show...no. Pet rescue...maybe...no. Another food show...God. She wonders how many cooking shows Guy Fieri is on. Resigned to what she needs to do, she turns off the TV. Out loud, but to herself, she says, "God!"

The Joy gets up and looks at herself in the mirror by the front door. She straightens her hair. The black spots are gone now. She thinks, "I'm straightening my hair for a phone call. I blame this behavior on my friendship with Steph." She glances at the clock, hopes for an outgoing message and out loud she says, "Here we go."

Ring tone. Then, over the phone comes Betty's voice, "Oh, my. You usually wait until you think I'll be at the club."

The Joy does her best surprised line read on, "What? Of course not." She doesn't even sound like herself. The Joy's speech is much more measured than her usual carefree pattern and she now sounds a bit like her mother.

Betty says, "Actually, you just caught me. I was flying out the door to meet the Harris's for a cocktail before dinner. Janey is visiting and they've invited me to join them. Isn't that thoughtful?"

"Oh, yes. Well, please tell them all I asked about them."

"And how is my one and only Joy?"

"I'm fine."

"I'm unconvinced."

"New York is not Florida, Betty. I haven't been golfing or playing tennis."

"That is awful. And *why* can't you call me Betz like everyone else?"

"I don't know."

After exhausting the appropriate amount of air, Betty asks, "Are you working? We've heard that non-essential businesses are closed up there."

"I'm working it out."

"And how about your diet? So many people are using this pandemic as an excuse to just shove whatever they want in their mouths. Like the calories won't count. It's disgusting. You should see Carol. You remember Carol Baker, her son used to tease you all the time. Remember? You wet your pants after the regatta and he called you Wee Wee Winters. Well, Carol has ballooned up to over...she must be over two hundred pounds by now."

Through gritted teeth, The Joy says, "I was five and the bathroom was locked."

"What?"

"Nothing...Tell me about you. How are you? It sounds like you're still able to maintain your social life."

"Yes, well...It's not the same. We've had to cancel our bridge games for now. Everyone's afraid to touch the cards, so my Wednesday nights are wide open...Oh, wait. I do have news."

"What's that?"

"Nathan Waxman, he's Jewish you know, invited me to join him on his patio last week for iced tea."

"You are the adventurer."

"Don't be smart...Anyway, then he invited me in to show me a painting he'd bought at the Sinclair auction. Well of course, I wasn't going to go in."

Feigning understanding, The Joy says, "Of course not."

"So he brought it out! He took it off of his wall, and walked it outside, just so I could enjoy it and not take a chance going into an enclosed space."

"That is something."

Betty is lost in her own thoughts, "I wonder where he thinks this will lead."

"Hmm."

Suddenly Betty sounds rushed, "Look at the time. I can't believe you've kept me this long. I have to run. I don't want to be rude to the Harris's. Thank you for the call. Try not to eat too much. Maybe try an online workout class. I'm doing Zumba, Pilates *and*...your mother is trying tai chi. It's very slow, but I really feel like I'm getting in touch with myself. Coronavirus is making me quite the adventurer."

"OK. Bye, Mom."

"Well, that sounds like you're done talking."

The Joy wonders why every call with Betty feels like a brand-new slap in the face. She presses forward, "Have a fun night, Betty. Happy Mother's Day."

Thrown by that, Betty says, "Oh, my word. Can you believe I forgot that it's Mother's Day? Here I thought you were just being thoughtful." Betty laughs to herself and the phone clicks off.

The Joy sits in the silence and flashes back to different moments from her youth. Her mind is suddenly clouded with a festival of disappointments, embarrassments, and failed attempts at fitting in. And Betty was always there to point out her missteps—always so obsessed with the thought that others would judge her by her daughter's inadequacies. Then, finally, Betty stopped trying to make Joy right, and just tried to make her distant. That seemed to work best for all involved.

The Joy doesn't even realize that she's shaking her head.

She's snapped out of her trip down memory lane by the sound of Kimi's curtain opening. The Joy sees Kimi standing there, holding The Joy's prized silver cocktail tray with two lovely martinis on it. Kimi is also wearing a face mask that says, "I just F*cked Your Mother."

SHAD & BENJI'S APARTMENT

Benji is on the sofa playing Nintendo Wii. He is one hundred percent all in. Nothing else exists. When his *Mario Kart* crosses the finish line, he thinks, "This is the best thing Mom could have sent...Mom. Oh shit! I need to call home."

Benji looks around and realizes that his laptop is in the loft. He heads up to retrieve it and a moment later comes back down and puts it on the coffee table. He sets up for a video call, then texts his mother to tell her to join. Benji sits still and stares at his screen for about six minutes before both of his parents join him. Mike and Dayna Mathews look about as middleclass as they come. He's wearing a polo style shirt with a logo from his tech company on the breast pocket. She has on a solid purple T-shirt that's too big for her. They're both decent-enough looking people, but do nothing to enhance that. Not being naked is enough.

They look good to Benji. "Dad, I didn't know you'd be joining us."

Mike says, "I miss you, buddy."

"Aw, that's so sweet...Happy Mother's Day, mom."

Dayna smiles, "Thank you, Benj...You look good."

"Thanks. You guys do, too. Hey, thanks for sending my Wii."

Dayna: "You bet."

"How are you guys?"

Dayna: "We're fine. As weird as anyone right now, I guess. We're worried about you."

"Why?"

Dayna: "We hear how bad it is in the city. The lines, the shortages, all those people catching it. You're not taking any chances, are you Benj?"

"No. Me and Shad are mostly just inside. I've been to the market a few times, but I wear my mask and gloves, and we wipe everything down before we put it away."

Dayna shakes her head and laughs to herself, "Shad. I just...I've had a lot of black students, but no one named Shad."

Mike gets in on the joking, "What kind of a name is Shad, really? It's like, excuse me. I have to go take a Shad."

Both Dayna and Mike laugh at once. Mike goes on, "Oh, crap. I think I just Shad my pants."

Dayna's loaded and ready to one-up him, "You mean, Oh Shad! I just Shad my pants." And, with that, it's very clear why this marriage works. Benji looks around to make sure his roommate is not in ear-shot.

Trying to hold back her laughter and to sound caring, Dayna asks, "How is Shad?" With that, she and Mike bust out uncontrollably. It takes a moment for them to regain most of their composure.

Benji waits, then, "He's great. Guess what? He's going to run a marathon...right here in the apartment."

Dayna: "You're kidding?"

"Yeah. I mean, no. We're raising money for charity. For restaurant workers. That part was my idea. And people are signing up. It's so cool."

Mike: "Wow."

"And, it's not just in the U.S. now. We've had these two guys up in Canada sign up. When we told them that we were just raising money for restaurant workers in America, because of taxes and laws, they said they didn't care."

Mike looks impressed. "I am really proud of you, Benj."

"Thanks."

Mike switches to a more serious tone, "Listen, buddy. Your mother and I think that maybe you should consider moving back down here with us for a little while. Until this thing passes. You're not working right now, so you'd be saving money and we think it's a lot safer down here. You can have your room, we have the big yard..."

Dayna adds, "We could binge *The Great British Baking Show* together."

Benji is blindsided by the offer. "I'm fine here. Really."

Dayna reasons, "Benj, I don't want to pull rank, but everything I'm hearing from my friends at Stanford say that you're not. And they don't see it changing in the foreseeable future. People don't get it. This is not going to be over at the end of the month...or next month. This could be years.

"You want me to move home for years?"

Mike waves his hands, "No...But would it be so bad? You'll be with people who love you.

Like only a mom can say, Dayna reasons, "We love you so much, Benj."

Mike: "And you'll be a lot safer here. Come on. Use your head, buddy. You're a smart guy. You know we're right."

There's a long silence as everyone waits for an answer. Benji looks around his apartment and thinks about his little life in New York. He has some friends. Not a lot, but some. He knows his restaurant friends just tolerate him. But Shad and the gang, they like him. Right?

Mike adds, "It's the right thing, buddy."

THE JOY'S APARTMENT

It's late and The Joy and Kimi are having a "Let It Go" party. They're on opposite ends of the sofa and they are hammered. There are no actual words coming out of either of them, just sounds. But this does not stop them from laughing their asses off. God, they need this.

STEPH'S APARTMENT

In her white tank top and a new pair of silk men's pajama bottoms, Steph walks from her bedroom into the dark kitchen. There's enough city light from the windows to make turning on more lights unnecessary. This is how she most likes her place. She pours herself a glass of red wine, gets her computer and puts both down on her coffee table. She's ready. Steph opens her mail and looks at the email from Janis at the top of her inbox. The subject line simply reads: Read this. Steph takes a sip of wine and clicks on the email. Here we go.

> Steph,
> I wonder how long it will take you to open this. Don't be too big a weenie. It won't bite you. Just read it.
>
> *I know that working for me wasn't easy. Thank you for never saying so. Although, it was often on your face. I want to share a few words of broadcast news wisdom. Hopefully, you'll heed them and they'll help you in your career (which, I fear might be big.)*
>
> *First, listen more than you speak. People will think you're thoughtful and smarter then you are. Next, keep copious notes on everything. You never know when you're going to have to back yourself up. Also, do more research then you think you're going to need. You're going to need it. Thank people for a job well done. Most people only reach out when there's a problem. This is how you'll create loyalty. Lastly, and perhaps most importantly, NEVER drink and text. It's a career killer.*
>
> *That's it. See, that wasn't so painful. Cheers to what could be a stellar career.*
>
> *Janis*

P.S. Don't be a douche

Steph sits back. Wow. After a moment, she leans forward and clicks, save as new.

SHAD & BENJI'S APARTMENT/SHAD'S BEDROOM

In his running togs, Shad is putting in miles on his treadmill. He has his laptop open and running a video of a past New York City marathon for inspiration. He also has in earbuds and is listening to his "Stay Pumped" play list. Shad checks his watch to monitor time and heart rate. He's a man on a mission.

SHAD & BENJI'S APARTMENT/BENJI'S LOFT

Benji's in bed staring at the ceiling. He's wearing headphones and listening to driving J-pop music. There's a lot to consider. Do his parents want him to come more because he's an only child and he's all they have? Do they think that he's not capable of getting through this on his own? He thinks, "I'm a man. I'm a full-grown man." Then he thinks about how sad his parents would be if something happened to him. What does he owe them? Answer: So much. More staring at the ceiling.

ZOOM SPILL

THE JOY'S APARTMENT

The Joy, in the same outfit as the night before, is carefully moving around the apartment, as if any misstep will cause everything to fall off the walls. Is this an entirely new level of hangover? Fuuuck. At the kitchen counter, she pulls out the box of Pop-Tarts and puts four of the pastries in the toaster. Slowly, she crafts two chocolate martinis. Why is this taking so long? It feels like the world has slowed down. Ugh! The toaster finally pops and she puts the treats on a tray with the drinks and a small bud vase. She slides everything, oh, so gingerly over to the computer and looks at her watch. It's time. She thinks, "Should I get Kimi? Too much work. Fuck her. This is her fault." The Joy gets on her bar stool and opens the laptop.

Kimi opens her curtain, mumbling, "I smell Pop-tarts." She shuffles over. Her first attempt at getting on the bar stool is unsuccessful. New approach. She climbs up by getting on her hands and knees on the stool and slowly turning until her butt carefully eases its way on to the seat. The Joy is fascinated by this maneuver. "I'll pay you if you can do that again."

Kimi answers flatly, "I can not."

The Joy gives an *Oh well* shrug and hits the appropriate computer keys to launch the call. They wait in silence.

The first window to show up has Shad, Benji and Douglas. They're clearly speaking, but The Joy and Kimi can't hear them."

Incredulously Kimi shakes her hands in the air. "Really. Have they really *still* not figured this out?"

The Joy points to the lower corner of the frame. "We can't hear you."

Kimi: "...You fucking idiots."

Shad, suddenly audible, "But we can hear you."

Kimi: "You know that was said with love."

Shad: "I know what it was said with."

Another screen comes up. It's Jackson. What the hell is he wearing? Is that an oxford shirt and glasses? That just makes no sense. In his usual, carefree manner, Jackson says, "Hello all!"

Shad: "Hello, sir. Do we know you?"

Jackson laughs as Steph's screen appears. She's in a new dark-blue blouse. "Am I late?"

Kimi: "Yes."

Steph: "Sorry. Work." She notices Jackson's attire and says admiringly, "Oh, Jackson. Look at you. Very scholarly."

Jackson: "Why, thank you."

Steph: "So did we all call our mothers?"

Without expression, The Joy says, "Fuck you."

Steph: "Wow. Someone's been living with Kimi too long."

Kimi: "Fuck you."

Steph: "I'll stop talking now."

The Joy: "Not everyone's parents think their children are amazing and can do no wrong."

Steph: "What? I'm a constant disappointment."

Kimi: "Bullshit."

Steph: "Seriously, my mother's constant refrain is, I'm disappointed, but I love you anyway. She says it even when she doesn't actually say it. You can feel it."

Kimi: Have you told her that you're an out-of-work lesbian yet?"

Steph: "No."

The Joy: "Have you told her that your weight is up and you lost your license?"

Steph: "No."

Shad: "Have you told your father that you're never going to be in the NFL?"

Steph is picking up on the trend. "No."

Kimi: "Then, we don't want to hear it."

Steph: "Wow. OK, then."

Benji blurts out, "My parents want me to move home."

That sits like a bomb. Everyone over-talks their surprise. Shad says, "But you're not going to, right?"

Benji: "I don't know. They say it's not safe for me to stay here. And I think they're afraid that their only child will die. They're really worried and I feel bad. They've done so much for me."

The gang is silent as they all think about Benji's news. Finally, Shad says, "When are you going to decide?"

Benji hugs Douglas and shrugs.

The Joy: "Well, this call is a big bummer."

Steph: "May I share a bit of positive news, or will you all dog-pile on me?"

The Joy: "You may."

Steph: "I got an email from Janis."

Jackson: "And what did Mrs. Drunk Texting have to say to you?"

Steph, "She gave me a few words of career advice, including not to drink and text, then told me to not be a douche."

Kimi: "That is positive."

Shad: "Wingman and I have positive news. Over a hundred people have signed up for the marathon so far. Benji, tell them."

Benji is slow to get started, but gains momentum, "At last check, we actually have one hundred, twenty-two. We now have four in Canada and one in Scotland. Jackson set up all the non-profit stuff and the tax stuff..."

Kimi: "Our Jackson?"

With a smile, Jackson says: "I appreciate your support."

Benji, "And he got Clif Bar to sponsor us."

The Joy is hungover but delighted: "That's amazing."

Benji: "Which part?"

The Joy: "All of it."

Shad: "So Steph, what do you say?"

Steph: "What do I say about what?"

Shad: "About making us a news story."

Steph: "I told you. I don't get to just decide what will be the news. The news is the news."

Shad: "A, that means nothing, and B, you said you'd ask. Couldn't you at least try?" There's a long silence as everyone shoots Steph their best, sad, puppy face.

Steph: "Seriously?" Another long pause. "Fine, I'll talk to Bill, but I'm promising nothing."

Shad: "That's great. That's all I'm asking. Squeaky wheel gets the oil. This is going to be so great. Wait till my father sees this. In your face, Joe!"

Steph tries to manage expectations. "There are no guarantees."

Shad tries to act casual but can't. "I know. I know. But it's gonna be great." Turning to Benji he says, "Right, Wingman?"

Benji: "Right."

The Joy: "Well, this call took an upturn. Cheers, me." She raises her glass and everyone else follows. "*Cheers!*" After a happy sip, The Joy says, "OK, then. Are we all ready?"

Kimi: "For what?

The Joy: "Oh, my God. To share a secret. Come on. You guys promised. Who wants to go first?" No one responds. They all drink and look at each other. "Oh, come on."

Jackson jumps in: "I'll take the lead."

The Joy claps with delight: "Oh, goody!"

Jackson: "I'm going back to law school."

Kimi: "Shut the fuck up."

Shad: "You went to law school?"

Jackson: "I did. But it wasn't right for me at the time. It's right now. I'll be studying law for non-profits. I've been accepted to NYU. They have one of the most comprehensive public interest law programs in the country. I start in September…And it won't affect my Ninja training."

Benji: "Congratulations."

Jackson: "Thank you, Benjamin."

Benji: "You're welcome. The force is strong with this one."

Kimi: "What the hell is happening?"

The Joy: "Our little Jackson is growing up."

Jackson: "Hopefully, not too much." Changing gears, Jackson says, "Oh, The Joy, I was considering your predicament. Understand, I would not give you this advice as a practicing lawyer, but I'm not a practicing lawyer so, I'm free to advise you on misconduct."

The Joy: "I already like this."

Jackson: "You do not need a license to cut a friend's hair if they are not paying you."

The Joy: "Now, I don't like this."

Jackson: "Just, walk the path with me for a moment. You cut a…" He makes air quotes "*…friend's* hair. They don't pay you, but they do give you a *gift*." More air quotes.

The Joy's wheels star turning, "Ooooooh. A gift. Nudge, nudge. Wink, wink."

Kimi: "Not that kind of gift, you whore."

The Joy's wheels turn in a better direction. "Ooooh…money."

Jackson: "You never say the M word. You just suggest a *gift*."

The Joy considers this. "And if they think I mean a *gift*…" Air quotes.

Kimi: "Oh, my God. Not everyone wants to screw you...Thank you Jackson for this very strange but helpful version of you."

The Joy: "Yes. Thank you, Jackson."

Jackson: "You are like my first dollar bill. Well, my second. Shad was my first."

Shad: "You never forget your first."

The Joy: "I try to." She shakes off that memory and says, "That was so good, Jackson. OK, who's next?"

Steph: "I'll go next. I'm sleeping with a law student." She winks at Jackson.

The Joy: "Yay! See how fun this is!"

Shad: "You know that we all kind of knew that one."

Steph: "But you weren't sure, so it counts."

The Joy: "I'm the judge, and I say it counts...Jackson, do you have anything else you want to share with Steph?"

A bit confused Jackson looks around and says, "No?"

The Joy: "OK. We'll leave it at that." No one else is willing to say anything and The Joy moves on. "Who's next?"

Shad: "Well, that is a hard act to follow. But, OK. I'm taking you back to high school."

Kimi: "Yes, let's all relive that pain."

Shad: "One morning, I got dressed for school in the dark. I shared a room with Chad and he was sick. I didn't want to wake him up. So I got up, put on white underwear, I *thought*, cream colored pants, a shirt, and left. All day, kids were walking behind me laughing. No idea why. I was like, did someone put a note on my back? Nope. So I just go on with my day. I get to football practice and I'm suiting up in the locker room, right? And I catch my ass in the mirror. What the hell's on my white underwear? Then I realize, I was wearing underwear with navy blue lettering that said, 'Juicy Ass!' Big, block letters that you could see through my cream-colored pants. I spent the whole day with 'Juicy Ass' across my butt. Oh, my God. So embarrassing."

Everyone has a good laugh at Shad's expense, including Shad. Kimi says, "Especially if juicy is false advertising."

Shad defends himself, "What? My ass is plenty juicy." More laughter.

Benji: "OK, Juice."

Steph: "You actually walked into a store and bought underwear that said, 'Juicy Ass'?"

Shad: "Well, no..." Preparing for the real confession, Shad pauses then says, "My mom bought them for me." With that, everyone loses it. Big, cleansing laughter. The kind that bends you over. Shad tries to defend his mother saying, "She thought it was cute." It takes a long while for the laughter to die down.

Jackson: "Thank you, Shad. You did not disappoint, my friend."

Benji announces, "I had a twin."

Everyone is startled. Shad turns to his roommate. "What?"

Benji: "I had a twin. A sister. Bonnie. A fraternal twin."

Steph: "My God. What happened?"

Benji: "She drowned. At the lake. We were three. She was there and then she wasn't. It was just one of those things."

Steph: "Benji, I'm so sorry." Everyone is quiet now, not knowing what to say."

Benji: "I think it's why my parents want me to come home. They're afraid of losing another kid. That would be really hard on them."

Steph: "I can't imagine."

Jackson: "We're all sorry. We didn't know."

Benji: "It's OK. I always think, maybe there's something I don't know about a person. You know? You never see everything. Maybe there's a reason for them being that way."

Kimi: "This is a great fuckin' game, Joy."

The Joy: "You forgot the, *The*."

Benji: "Wait, I have another one. I was born with six toes on one foot."

Well, that was a one-eighty. But one that everyone is happy to embrace. Excitedly, The Joy claps and bounces on her stool. "Show and tell. Let's see it."

Benji pulls off his right shoe and sock and holds his foot up to the computer. The gang all leans in for a closer look. Benji explains, "It's not really a full toe. It's like an extra, midget, pinky toe."

Shad: "How do I not know this?"

Benji: "It's all about maintaining some mystique."

Shad: "You definitely have your own mystique."

Benji playfully raises his eyebrows multiple times to enhance his *mystique*.

The Joy: "Kimi, want to go?"

Kimi: "No."

The Joy: "Fine. I'll go. OK, I... have been sleeping with Vlad, my PackageGuys guy."

In unison, everyone says: "We know."

The Joy: "Really? OK. Fine. Wait. OK. Don't tell Vlad. I slept with the mail man."

In unison, everyone says, "Yeah. We know that too."

The Joy: "Wow. You guys are making this really hard...OK. Got it. I don't have a cat."

Kimi: "What?!"

The Joy: "I made up The Fred."

Kimi is completely taken aback. "Who has an imaginary pet?"

The Joy: "I always wanted a cat, but I'm allergic."

After a beat, Kimi says: "I'm engaged."

Wow. No one saw that coming, either. Everyone reels at the news. Crazy-excited Steph says, "When did this happen?"

Kimi: "Has anyone else noticed that when there's a question to be asked, it's always Steph? Two days ago. She asked and I accepted. She thinks she's marrying a face mask mogul. I'm gonna be a bride."

Kimi gets a huge round of congratulations that goes on for a while. Then, The Joy has a realization, "Does that mean you're moving out?"

Kimi: "And leave all this? I guess. Eventually. But Carmen's stuck in Florida for now. We haven't made any actual *plan* plans. We just know we want to keep it small. A few friends and you assholes. Correction. You, juicy assholes."

The Joy: "Wait. Does everyone have something to drink?"

Steph: "Who do you think we are?"

The Joy lifts her glass, as do the rest. "A toast. To a lawyer, a marathoner, a man with an extra toe, a news lady with a sexy sex toy, a bride to be and a very lucky roommate..."

Kimi: "The best roommate."

The Joy: "Cheers."

NEW DAY IN PARADISE

STEPH'S APARTMENT

Steph is staring into her fridge. Nothing is calling her name. She steps away and looks out the window to the city. There's a siren in the distance. She can't make out where it's coming from. It just feels like part of the view now. After a while, she heads back to the fridge and opens the door. Nothing has changed. She wonders why part of her expects to find something new. Steph finally grabs a small container of almond milk and goes to the computer.

Her cell rings. It's Bill. She answers, "Yeah, Bill."

"How come you never say, good morning?"

"I'm sorry. Good morning, Bill. How are you?"

"Very well. Thanks for asking."

There's a bit of a silence. Steph is waiting for an answer about covering Shad's story, but doesn't want to be the one to bring it up. Finally, Bill says, "You're not going to ask, are you?"

Steph knows Bill has her number, "You found me out."

"So I talked to Mason, and he likes the story. Solid human interest and we can do the whole thing without going into homes and breaking any protocols. It's still a megillah. We have a few elite athletes in the mix. We're going to want to cover them for sure. Then we want to make sure we get a few solid human interest stories to follow...cancer survivors, restaurant workers trying to get by, hard-luck stories...If we can get a runner that is a COVID survivor, that would be great. I want you to do most of the leg work. I'm giving you Jackie and Teddy to help with that... Say, thank you, Bill."

"Thank you, Bill."

Bill continues explaining the procedure to be followed with a military-like precision. "Each story we cover will need to have someone living in the residence to capture it. Not someone from outside. We'll give you the tech info to pass on to them, along with best practices for framing, lighting, things like that. We want to avoid logos on shirts and hats. We'll check all the feeds the day before. You're going to cover the entire event from your apartment. I like that wall of windows you have as backdrop. They face South. That's good. We'll air the tee-up story, the start, a few moments during with some backstories, the first few finishers, and we'll get your organizer, Shad Perkins, finishing. We're already talking to marketing about getting some promos together.

Bill finally stops talking. There's a moment of silence as Steph absorbs all of this. Bill, "Say, thank you, Bill."

"Thank you, Bill."

"Thank you. It's a good story."

THE JOY'S APARTMENT

The Joy is standing at her open front door with Beatrice and her daughter. This time, Beatrice is in a graphic black and white swing-top. It matched her black and white mask, from the On Your Face Mask collection. Her daughter is wearing one as well.

The Joy peeks her head into the hallway and looks in both directions. No one. Still, she speaks loudly as if for the benefit of a hidden mic, "So Beatrice, it's been too long. It was so great to visit with friends again."

Beatrice catches on. She responds with equal volume, "Yes. You're such a good friend. We all need friends now." She smiles at The Joy and winks. Mission accomplished. Before she leaves, she leans to The Joy. In a much lower tone she says, "I'll Venmo you that *gift* as soon as I get home."

The Joy says, "Oh. I love gifts."

"And please tell Kimi that we love the masks." She looks at her daughter's mask which reads, "My Other Mask Says, Fuck Off!" She then chuckles to herself and says, "They're just so cute."

"I'll tell her."

Beatrice says, "Love you."

With that, mother and daughter head down the hall and out. They Joy again looks side to side down her building hallway. No one's there. She closes the door and smiles. She says to herself, "I love having friends."

SHAD & BENJI'S APARTMENT/SHAD'S BEDROOM

Shad is wearing a business shirt, running shorts and sneakers. He jogs in place with his cell to his ear. He's in mid-client call. "I can't answer that Janet. It really depends how much you think you're going to need access to in the next, let's say, six months to a year."

Janet answers, "I don't think we need to touch any of it. I mean, you never know. I think if I keep a hundred to the side..."

"So you want to put the other eight-handle back in play?"

"I guess I'd be comfortable with that."

Shad keeps jogging, but looks over at Janet's account info which is up on his computer. "That puts you almost a full mill. in. We won't do it all at once. Ten to twenty a week. There's going to be a lot of volatility but we think there's going to be a lot of opportunity coming up as well."

Janet adds, "By the way, I went online and made a donation to your race. It's such a great cause. I've been telling my friends they *have to* donate."

Shad stops jogging. He's sincerely touched. "Janet, that's so nice. I so appreciate that."

"You're doing a great thing. A little crazy, but great."

"Thank you...And I'll start getting that money moved over tomorrow."

"Fantastic."

The call ends. Shad thinks for a moment about people, strangers, donating to the race. He wonders if his father will donate, then resumes his jogging.

JACKSON'S APARTMENT

Jackson is in his hallway, in his silk pajama pants. They look a lot like the ones Steph now likes to wear. He's behind his mini-tramp. He takes four measured steps back and stops. Then, with a burst of energy, he runs forward, hits the tramp and flies into position, deftly stopping himself off the ground with his hands and feet. Now in place, he checks the time, then reaches over to his high shelf and grabs his phone. Now solidly propped up, he signs in as admin on the race sign-up page and reviews the signup list, as well as the take so far. This is good.

THE JOY'S APARTMENT

Kimi watches The Joy escort another "friend" into her bedroom/salon. This time it's a very mod looking Asian woman in her seventies. Her Lilly Pulitzer dress matches her mask. Kimi shakes her head and wonders why she ever thought that not having a license would stop that woman.

Kimi hears a bit of a commotion out front and goes to the window. She looks down and sees that in the line to the market below, a posturing match has broken out. A squat guy in a leather vest and American flag T-shirt is puffing his chest up at a bookish-looking fellow, dressed for a day at the library. Kimi opens the window to hear better.

The Bookish Guy is saying, "It was a mistake. I just forgot it."

Mr. Leather Vest yells, "How do you forget your damn mask?"

This could get good. Kimi pulls out her phone to video the scene. She's not the only one.

Bookish Guy tries to explain, "Look, I just want to get some soy milk. Then I'm gone."

Mr. Leather Vest puffs up his chest. "No. You're gone now."

With that, Bookish Guy shrinks. "It was an honest mistake. I'm not trying to cause any trouble."

"Too late."

"I just need to get milk for my kid."

Lemon Lady #1 calls out, "Does anyone have an extra mask for this guy? Anyone?"

Mr. Leather Vest stomps his foot, "Get the fuck out of here!"

Kimi ducks back into the apartment. She quickly goes to her corner and sifts through a few masks that are on her La-Z-Boy. No. No. No. This one! She grabs it and rushes back to the window just as it looks like things might come to blows. Calling out she yells, "Wait! Wait! I have a mask for you. I have a mask."

The commotion stops as the people in line look up at Kimi. She's waving a mask. Bookish Guy sheepishly walks over to the window. Kimi says, "Catch." She tosses the mask to him and he catches it. He calls up, "Thank you." He puts it on and steps quietly in line.

Mr. Leather Vest looks at him and then at the mask, which reads, "I suck less with a mask." Mr. Leather Vest laughs, looks up at Kimi and yells, "You got that right, lady."

Kimi yells back, "I'm no lady."

Several people in line laugh. Lemon Lady #1 looks up at Kimi. Kimi wonders if under her mask, Lemon Lady #1 is smiling at her. No way to know. The moment is broken when a text vibrates Kimi's phone. The text is from Carmen., "Hey you."

Kimi texts back, "Hey, yourself. You won't believe what just happened."

"???"

"I think one of my masks just saved a life."

"My hero."

"No. You."

"Tell me what I'm thinking."

"That I'm gonna be a raging success as an entrepreneur."

"Of course, you are. Guess again."

"Use your words."

"You're no fun."

"That's why you love me."

"I'm thinking you should move to Miami."

Wow. Kimi didn't see that coming. She leaves the window and shuffles to her corner. She closes the curtain and gets in her La-Z-Boy. What to say?

Carmen texts again, "???"

Kimi replies, "Thinking."

"Thinking good or thinking bad?"

"Thinking."

"This should be an easy one. You're living on a La-Z-Boy."

"But my business is starting to take off."

"It's online. You can do that from anywhere."

Kimi doesn't know what to say. Yes. She is living on a chair. Not something most people aspire to. Hell, she didn't aspire to it. But she's just starting to adjust to her life. Things are working. Changing it up now could change her juju. Fuck.

Again Carmen texts, "???"

STEPH'S APARTMENT/BEDROOM

Steph is laying on her back on top of the covers. Her head is propped up and she's got "The Morning Show" on without sound. Her focus is on her phone. She's talking to Jackson.

"You gave everyone quite a surprise."

Jackson says, "I like surprises. Don't you?"

"When I can plan for them."

"I like that they're worried about you. Because I'm such a bad boy."

"You are bad. Why don't you tell them about Ruby?"

"This is more fun. It gives them something to do besides play video games and re-watch old sci-fi."

"You play video games and re-watch old sci-fi."

"True. But I can handle it."

"You're a renaissance man."

"Your renaissance man."

"Hmm."

"Now that I'm going to be a proper professional, would you tell your parents about me?"

Steph laughs. After too much silence, she asks, "You were serious?"

"Of course."

"How can everything be so, of course, for you?"

"Resistance only creates friction."

"You're full of shit."

"I'm not."

"You're not. Are you?"

"Well… perhaps on occasion."

Steph is feeling like perhaps this just got way more serious that it was two minutes ago. How the hell did this happen? Does it even matter? It happened. Right then, she sees an incoming call from Ida. Saved! In a rush, she says, "It's Ida. I gotta go."

Before Steph can bolt away, Jackson tosses out, "Tell her I said, hello."

"Talk to you later."

Steph sits up on the bed, readies herself and answers the call. Feigning casualness, she says, "Hey, Mom."

Ida says, "Hey yourself. I was wondering if you were ignoring me."

"What? No. I was on a work call."

"It's always a work call. Maybe one day it will be a boyfriend call. Are you still seeing someone?"

"Hmm…What's up?"

"I see. We're changing the topic. Fine. I called to tell you that I've been working on myself."

"Really?"

"What? I'm not too old to work on myself? And this is a complement for you. Because of what you did for that woman. Mrs. Moore. It was such a beautiful thing and I thought, I need to be a better person. So I wanted to let you know that I've gotten rid of my shit list."

"Wow, Mom. That's gr…"

"But I still remember who was on it."

Steph laughs out loud. "You know that's not how it works."

"What?"

"If you're still thinking about people as being on your shit list, the fact that the paper is gone is meaningless. You still have the list in your head."

After a moment, Ida laughs, as well. "Here I thought I was being a better person. Turns out I'm the same louse I always was." More laughing.

"Well, Mom, knowing is half way to a cure."

Playfully Ida says, "And that's all I need. Half way."

"At least you can laugh about it. Listen, Mom…"

"I know. You want to get off the phone with your mother."

"No, I…"

"That's OK. But one thing. Since you're going to do that story for your friends, have you thought any more about doing a story about your aunt's challah?

"Bye, Mom. I love you."

"I love you, too."

Steph sits on her bed and watches "The Morning Show" in silence.

SHAD & BENJI'S APARTMENT

Benji, in a new anime shirt, is in the kitchen working on a large pot of chili. Douglas is by his side, ever hopeful. Benji tastes what he's created so far and thinks. What does it need? He adds a hit of fish sauce and tastes it again. Better. After putting the lid back on, he looks at Douglas. Benji grabs the loaf of crusty bread that's sitting on the counter and rips off a small piece for Douglas. "Here, boy. Have a piece of Fluffers."

Douglas is happy with the offering. Might there be more? No. OK. Douglas goes to the living room, spins three times and settles on his mat. Shad walks into the living room. He's in his current uniform of business shirt and running shorts.

Benji sees him, "Hey man. Want some chili? It'll be better tomorrow, but it's pretty good now."

"Sure. Hit me."

Benji fills two bowls with chili and, while shredding some cheese over them, he calls out, "How much cheddar?"

"Make it rain."

Benji then rips two more pieces off of Fluffers, rests one on top of each bowl and joins Shad on the sofa. "Here you go."

As they eat, Shad absently says, "Ever wonder why we have a dinner table?"

"We like to watch TV while we eat."

"It's not even on."

Benji reaches for the remote and clicks on the TV. "We like to watch TV while we eat."

With a touch of irony, Shad says, "Oh, that's right." He lets a bit of time go by without words. Finally, "Have you made any decisions?"

Benji is now sucked into the TV and the young warriors fighting for what's right. Shad's voice is coming from a distant land. He mumbles, "What?"

"What have you decided?"

Benji answers from his trance with his eyes still on the screen, "I decided to be a cook...I decided I'm a shitty driver...I decided lots of things."

Frustrated, Shad puts down his bowl and claps his hands in front of Benji's face, hoping to get his actual attention. "Sunshine! over here."

Benji turns to Shad a bit annoyed, "I'm watching."

"I'm trying to find out if you're moving back to Jersey. Have you made a decision?"

"No." With that, Benji's attention goes back to his show. Shad picks up his bowl and heads back to his bedroom.

THE JOY'S APARTMENT

The Joy, now with pink hair, is at the kitchen counter with her computer open. She absently spoons from a large bowl of who-knows, while she reviews her calendar. It's filled with appointments that are entitled, "Friends." She then goes to her Venmo account. Look at that! She can't keep her excitement to herself. She calls out, "Kimi girl! Come look at this." She's still staring at the pretty numbers when Kimi shows up at her side.

Completely nonplussed, Kimi says, "Pink. OK."

"Yes. But no. Look." The Joy points to her computer. As Kimi leans to the screen to see what her roommate is seeing, she takes a spoon from The Joy's bowl and eats.

"Look at this. I'm actually on track to make more money from *gifts* from *friends* then I did when I was charging clients. Can you believe it? I'm so happy. I am literally filled with Joy." She thinks about that last statement for a moment and muses, "Does that make me a cannibal?"

Dryly, Kimi says, "Yes."

"Seriously?"

"How do you lose your license and make more money than ever?"

"So you weren't serious?"

"Oh, my God."

Thinking out loud, The Joy says, "People are actually gifting me more than I charge. People are so fascinating." She turns to Kimi, "Aren't people just fascinating?"

Kimi blurts, "Why don't you use your new-found wealth to go buy cat food? Oh, wait. That's right. You don't have a cat. Hey, more money for you!" Kimi goes and drops herself on the sofa. She pulls out her phone and looks at her text thread from Carmen. Fuck. After a moment, she texts Steph one word, "Question," and waits for a response.

Steph texts back, "What's up?"

"What if you wore one of my masks on TV for the race?"

"I won't be wearing a mask."

"Good for you."

"That all?"

"Yep."

Kimi sits motionless for a while. She farts and does nothing to try to hide it.

The Joy makes a face. "Hey!"

"What—that wasn't fascinating enough for you?"

SHAD & BENJI'S APARTMENT/SHAD'S BEDROOM

Shad's at his computer on an end-of-day team call. He's wearing a work shirt and running shorts. Max is on a long rant about Home Depot stock. While there's always a status review, the end-of-day calls have turned into pre-pump sessions for the next day. Like a coach's locker room speech to get the players ready to hit the field. Shad doesn't mind...much.

Max finishes his pep-talk and changes gears. He loses none of his intensity, "So we all know that Shad's charity run is coming up. We know he's going to be swift of foot and represent our team like a champion. And so, in honor of our teammate, I've made a sizable donation to his cause. And...I'd like the team to rise."

Everyone on the call stands up and Shad sees that while his teammates are all dressed for work from the waste up, they are all wearing running shorts, including Max. Then, they all reveal that under their work shirts they're wearing T-shirts with the race logo on them. Shad reflexively puts his hand on his heart. This is an unexpected gesture. The team claps for him.

Max adds, "Shad, my only advice is, run happy...and don't fuck up."

THE NIGHT OF

STEPH'S APARTMENT

The TVs are on in the background while Steph's attention is at her computer. She's going over her notes for the race. She wants to be as familiar as possible with all the runners and restaurant workers she's going to be covering. It's a good group. She's got her male and female elite athletes who have both run the Boston marathon and are expected to be the winners for their gender. She also has a woman in her forties who survived a car accident and was told she'd be lucky to walk again. A chef who'd just opened his restaurant, only to have it close a month later. The real heart story is the father and son who will be running together but separately. The son, in his late teens, is here in New York while Dad is a Navy pilot on an aircraft carrier in the Philippine Sea. And, of course, Shad she knows all too well. She thinks, best leave out the juicy ass underwear story.

Just then a promo comes on the TV for the race. It's a slow, heart-felt montage. Still shots of empty restaurants, cooks and servers, followed by a faster montage of photos of the race participants. It ends with her photo and an invitation to join her at the starting line, tomorrow.

Steph sits back and thinks, what am I wearing? She gets up and goes to her bedroom. She opens the closet doors and stares in. It's like staring into the fridge. No surprises. She feels her phone vibrate. It's Jackson, texting, "What are you going to wear tomorrow?"

"Right?"

"Wear your new dark blue blouse and the simple silver chain."

"You don't think I should look sporty?"

"It's your brand."

Steph considers the advice and is pleased to think, "I have a brand." She's going places. Well, without actually going places.

"You're going to be great."

"That's my job."

"Want me to call and say goodnight?"

"No. Too in my head. I'll just sound stupid."

"Stupid can be cute."

"You would know [wink emoji]"

"Ow."

"Didn't you see the [wink emoji]?"

"See you tomorrow [wink emoji]"

"[TV emoji]"

"[heart emoji]"

Steph wishes he didn't sent the heart emoji. She'd been avoiding heart emojis. Too much going on to think about that now. She'll think about that after the race.

KIMI'S CORNER

Kimi is in her La-Z-Boy. She's changed from her red winter hat to a red bucket hat, and she's bundled up in a cream-colored throw blanket. The overall effect is that she looks like a cocktail frank. She's reading *Anna Karenina* on her phone, but can't focus. Is it that it's ridiculously hard to get into Russian literature, or is she just an idiot? She'd picked it, thinking it would be a COVID accomplishment...Fuck Mrs. Karenina.

She decides to swipe the book aside and check her website for sales. Drum roll...What the what? That can't be right. She gets unwrapped, with a fair amount of difficulty, grabs her computer from the top of the box fridge and slides one butt cheek back onto the La-Z-Boy. The admin page is already up. Holy Shit! Where is this traffic coming from? She hashtags InYourFaceMasks and scans the results. There's a video. She clicks on it. It's the fight from in front of her apartment with Bookish Guy and Mr. Leather Vest. Someone posted the video with a link to her page. She watches it four times, maybe five and calls out, "I'm a mogul!"

SHAD & BENJI'S APARTMENT

The apartment is dark. Neither roommate is in the living area. Light from Shad's bedroom seeps out under the door. Low base tones seep down from Benji's loft. After a while, Shad Shuffles into the living room, wearing a T-shirt from a previous race, and sits on the sofa. He stares at nothing. He's having a million thoughtless thoughts. God, he hates the night before a race. He can never sleep.

Shad looks up at Benji's loft. The low beat signals that Benji might be awake. Shad decides to climb up and see if he has a late-night compatriot. He knocks on the railing.

Benji says, "Password."

"Dick face."

"Enter."

Shad finds Benji stretched out on his bed. He's never noticed before that Benji is actually too long for his mattress. Benji pulls off his headphones without turning off his music. The Japanese song leaks out.

Shad sits in Benji's chair. "Can't sleep."

Without much energy expense, Benji looks at his watch, "It's 2 a.m. You should try."

"I can't force it." They sit in silence for a while.

Benji props himself up on his elbows. "I'm staying."

Shad has to let the words sink in for a second before he realizes what Benji just told him. He's tired, but excited. "Really?"

"Yeah."

"That's so cool. What made you decide to stay?"

"I can't leave you without a wingman."

Shad is totally touched. He looks at his roommate and feels closer to this goofy, awkward white guy than he does to his own brothers. How weird is that? "How'd your parents take it?"

"I assume they'll keep trying."

"Can I ask why you're really staying? I mean, I just need a wingman tomorrow morning."

Benji sits up and crosses his long legs and thinks for a moment. Finally, "My dad calls me buddy a lot. I mean, I don't know. He's been calling me buddy forever. It was fine when I was like ten, but now...it just feels like every time he calls me buddy he's saying, 'Hey, I don't see you as a full-grown man who doesn't need his parents hovering over everything he does.' You know what I mean?"

"Yeah...well, I'm glad you're staying."

"Me, too." After a thoughtful silence, Benji says, "Go to bed."

"See you in the morning, Wingman."

"It is technically morning, buddy."

Shad smiles and leaves. Maybe he can sleep now.

RACE DAY

SHAD & BENJI'S APARTMENT/BENJI'S LOFT

In the dark, the phone alarm sounds. Benji hits it off and lays there for a quick moment. He swings his legs over and off the bed. He gets up, pulls off his pajamas and pulls on the T-shirt and shorts that were neatly folded on his bureau. Next comes his sneakers and a whistle. He has no actual plan for the whistle other than, he likes its official vibe. He jumps in place for a moment, then heads for the ladder.

SHAD & BENJI'S APARTMENT/SHAD'S BEDROOM

A whistle sounds outside Shad's door. Seems it didn't take long for Benji to find a use for it. Shad rubs his eyes and gets up. He opens his door to find Benji taking up the entire space. He's in his *We Are One Race, Marathon-In-Place* shirt.

With a good amount of sleep in his voice, Shad says, "OK. Let's do this."

STEPH'S APARTMENT

The sun's not up yet, but Steph is. She's getting in her last Peloton mile of the morning. It's a fast mile. She needs to burn off energy and feel like she's already earned a win before she gets on the air. Done!

She pedals slowly as the bike registers her stats. She grabs her water bottle and sips as she pedals. She'd thought about moving the bike into the bedroom last night because it will need to be out of frame for the shoot. But she likes her view too much, even in the dark.

After she cools down, she gets off the bike and walks to the kitchen. She stands as straight as possible. Posture is so important. On the counter, her phone blinks with a message. It's from Jackson and simply reads, "You are steely."

KIMI'S CORNER

Kimi is back in cocktail-frank mode and fast asleep. She dreams of countless number eights floating all around her like fireflies. It's her first good dream since before lock-down.

THE JOY'S APARTMENT/BEDROOM

The Joy sleeps peacefully until the sound of something in the apartment crashing to the floor semi-wakes her. She mumbles, "Darn that cat."

STEPH'S APARTMENT

The door buzzer is going off. Steph, dressed for air...except in her bare feet, scoots out of her bedroom to the front door, looks through the key hole and sees Davis wearing a smiley-face mask and burdened with as much equipment as one capable man can carry. He does not look happy to be so over-loaded. She lets him in, catches her breath and says, "Coffee?"

"Definitely. I've only had three cups so far."

Steph goes to the kitchen and puts a new cup in the Keurig. "How do you take it?"

"However I can get it?" He places his many bags on the floor and scans the apartment saying, "Decent digs."

"Thanks...Bill wants us to use the window as a backdrop."

"Whatever the boss wants."

Steph joins Davis by the windows and hands him a coffee. He asks, "Will there be more?"

"I'm loaded for bear."

"And no one here is pregnant, right?" He winks at her, which bathes her in relief. Davis drains his coffee in one long pull and hands back the mug for a refill. "It's gonna be great."

SHAD & BENJI'S APARTMENT

Benji does final apartment pick up. He usually doesn't care how the place looks, but his parents will be watching. Shad, now in a shirt that matches Benji's, is stretching and trying to get his muscles warm. He looks at the time.

Anxiously, Shad says, "You have all the lights ready?"

"Check."

"Your phone is fully charged?"

"Check."

"My phone is fully charged?"

"Check. And I've got your nutrition ready, your electrolytes, ibuprofen if you need it, and I've been in touch with Steph's guy. We tested everything. We're good to go. All you have to do is run."

"I have to go to the can again." Shad heads to the bathroom.

Benji calls out, "Don't miss the start."

THE JOY'S APARTMENT

The Joy and Kimi are individually wrapped in their blankets and on either end of the sofa. This is their position for the start of the race. They both have bowls of soup warming their hands.

The Joy is pleased with this new treat. "I wouldn't have thought of soup for breakfast."

"Ramen is good any time."

"This is so exciting."

"And all we have to do is sit here. Cheers." They clink soup bowls.

STEPH'S APARTMENT

All of the lighting is in place. Davis is ready. Steph is on her mark, looking perfect. She asks Davis, "How do I look?"

"Perfect."

With that, she puts her nerves on the shelf for the rest of the morning and thinks, "I'm steely." Davis gives her the count down, "In five, four, three..." He uses his fingers to signal, two, one...go.

To camera, Steph begins, "Good morning. This is Stephanie Weiss, Channel 7 News, bringing you live coverage of the first ever, *We Are One, Marathon In Place,* benefitting restaurant workers across the country. This was the brain-child of three friends from high school who wanted to find a way to use their COVID time to effect positive change. Shad Perkins, Benjamin Mathews, and Jackson Asghar have enlisted participants from all over the country and beyond. Elite athletes, casual runners, a woman who was told she'd be lucky to walk again, a father running with his son virtually from the deck of an aircraft carrier and a lot of folks who are excited to be doing something to help others. All of these runners will begin and end their race in their own homes. That's twenty-six point two miles, all at home. We'll be covering the start, the finishes and sharing a few of the athletes' amazing stories. Have you been missing the drama of sports? Are you wondering how you can help others? Looking for a positive story about the best side of us. Then stay tuned and watch it all unfold. And if you'd like to donate, go to WeAreOneMarathonInPlace.org. It's up on the screen and there's a link on our website. Again, all the money will go to support the restaurant workers of America. And it all starts, right after this commercial.

SHAD & BENJI'S APARTMENT

Shad's in position for the start, jumping straight up and down. From
behind his camera,
Benji says, "Ready champ?"

"Ready, wingman." Shad thinks about how much he hopes his father
watches him cross the finish. Then he thinks, hope is not a strategy.

JACKSON'S APARTMENT

Jackson is in the media room in a recliner. He's got on his race T-shirt and pajama pants. A bowl of popcorn sits on his lap. In his cup-holder is an energy drink. The large screen is on channel 7. Steph comes back on.

Steph: "Welcome back to the start of the *We Are One, Marathon in Place 2020*. I'm Stephanie Weiss and I'll be sharing all of the action with you. And we are about to start in..."

The TV screen cuts to a grid of frames, like a zoom call. In each window, there's a runner waiting to start. People in apartments, backyards and a man on the deck of an aircraft carrier in the dark. Steph's voice continues, "Three, two, one...They're off!"

Everyone on the TV starts running. Around sofas, in place, across yards. Within the grid, frames cut from runner to runner. It's a strangely intimate cross-section of humanity. Over the images, Steph's voice says, "It has begun. Accountants, dancers, realtors, bakers, electricians, construction workers, members of the military, health care workers, money managers, lawyers, dry cleaners, homemakers, all running to support our restaurant workers. We'll be checking back with the runners in a bit. Up next we talk with the creators of this very special race."

Jackson leans back and calls out, "Ruby. I'm going to be on TV. Come watch."

THE JOY'S APARTMENT

Kimi and The Joy have not moved from their spots on the sofa. As if to convince herself, The Joy says, "Well, this is exciting."

Kimi considers this and shrugs, "Eh."

Ok, so The Joy isn't alone in her lack of enthusiasm. She asks, "Bloodies?"

Kimi brightens, "Now I'm excited."

STEPH'S APARTMENT

Davis gives Steph the signal and she begins. "Welcome back to the *We Are One, Marathon in Place 2020*. I'm Stephanie Weiss and up next is an interview with the creators of the race, recorded earlier.

JACKSON'S APARTMENT

From his lounge chair, Jackson calls out again, "Ruby! Your brother is on TV. You're going to miss it."

Ruby, a young woman who looks related to Jackson but somehow not with his level of attractiveness, skulks into the room. She's dressed all in black, including her makeup. Goth? Not quite. She's holding a box of cigarettes and asks, "Have you been smoking?"

"What? No. Of course not. Sit. Sit, and watch your brother."

With zero enthusiasm, Ruby slips into a seat and looks at the TV. Shad and Benji are on the screen. They're on their sofa, wearing their race Ts, with Douglas between them. On the bottom of the frame are subtitles with their names and professions. Ruby says, "I don't see you."

"Shh. Wait."

On the TV, Shad is saying, "As we discussed it, it grew organically. We each kept making the other person's idea better. Bigger. Jackson was the one who made it really big."

The TV cuts to Jackson. Wow, the camera likes him.

Watching himself, he bursts with excitement and hits his sister on her arm. So much less excited, Ruby lights a cigarette and watches.

On screen, Jackson is subtitled as a law student. He says, "When Shad told me what he was attempting, I thought, this could be important. There's a way to truly help people here. Then Benjamin was the one who solved that next puzzle."

The TV cuts to Benji. "I'm a restaurant worker. I cook. So it wasn't hard to think of helping restaurant workers. I'm lucky to have my family's support and some savings, but not everybody has that, you know."

The TV cuts back to Steph in her apartment. "Quite an impressive group of young men. When we come back, we'll check in with the runners."

Beaming, Jackson turns to Ruby. "How about that? I'm an impressive young man."

Ruby keeps smoking, gets up and leaves the room.

SHAD & BENJI'S APARTMENT

Shad is jogging around the sofa. Benji is watching and eating a large sandwich. The bread seems barely able to contain all of the contents. He calls out with a full mouth, "That's twenty." With that, Shad changes directions around the sofa.

STEPH'S APARTMENT

Steph is speaking to camera, "Welcome back to the *We Are One, Marathon in Place 2020*. I'm Stephanie Weiss. Let's check in with our runners."

Steph looks at the large screen in front of her that shows what the home audience is seeing and listens to the feed of information coming through her earpiece.

THE JOY'S APARTMENT

The Joy and Kimi, each holding Bloody Marys loaded with more bacon then Mary, are now contented watching the race. They see frames with people running; some have family members walking through frame and waving, some have animals sitting and watching, some are utterly alone. One beefy guy is running in a bunny suit.

Steph's voice announces, "Up next, an interview recorded earlier with Vickie Cole, a woman just happy to be in the running."

The TV cuts back and forth from Steph to Vickie. Vickie is a woman is in her mid-forties and quite thin. She's on her sofa in a pastel yellow room. There's nothing remarkable about her until she speaks. "No one ever thought I'd be here. Not like this."

Steph points out, "You were hit by a driver who'd fallen asleep at the wheel."

"That's right," Vickie adds. "I woke up with five broken bones, including my pelvis. I was in a body cast for six months. After that, the doctors said, maybe I could walk again with a walker. Maybe. And I thought, no. You don't get to decide that for me. So that was the beginning. Every day, my goal was to take one more step than the day before. And that's what I did. Every day, another step. Then I started jogging those steps. When I heard about this race I thought, I can do that. I'll be in my own home."

At that moment, a young girl of about four jumps into her lap. Vickie hugs her and keeps talking. "I'll have my support right here. I can do it. And, I can help other people. So for me, just starting this race will be a victory." Vicky looks down at her daughter and hugs her again.

With that, both Kimi and The Joy have tears running down their faces.

The Joy asks Kimi, "Are you crying?"

"Shut up."

JACKSON'S APARTMENT

Jackson is alone again, which he assumes is how he will remain for the rest of the race coverage. He watches different runners as Steph reports on who's in the lead and how some of the key people, including Shad are doing. He's well behind the elites, but holding his own.

Next on the TV, Steph introduces the story of the Navy Pilot and his son. There's a split screen. On one side is the son. He's seventeen and in the family's apartment in Brooklyn. He's flanked by Mom and his two younger brothers. They all share the same face. On the other side of the screen is Dad, in uniform standing in front of a plane. The boy talks about how much he misses his dad and how proud he is of him. And how maybe, he'll beat his dad's time. Dad talks about how special it is to be able to share this accomplishment with his boy, even though they're so far away. And maybe his old man might be able to pull out the win.

After the interview, Steph shows how father and son are doing in the race. As his family cheers, the son is racing back and forth in a narrow strip of backyard. It's a strange juxtaposition with Dad running the landing strip of the aircraft carrier. But for Dad, it's nighttime. It seems like every member of the crew is out on deck, cheering him along. Dad's in the lead.

SHAD & BENJI'S APARTMENT

Not much has changed other than Shad's shirt is sweatier and Benji's sandwich is gone. Benji calls to Shad, "And, that's twenty."

Shad turns and runs in the other direction. He grabs a water bottle as he goes by and takes a sip. Benji checks the TV and reports, "Sharon just finished. Three hours, twenty-seven minutes. Wow!"

Shad runs and talks, "She made great time."

"You're doing great, too, man."

THE JOY'S APARTMENT

The Joy and Kimi have fallen asleep on the sofa. A truck backfires and wakes Kimi up. She does a long blink and tries to reorient. She looks from the clock to the TV, then gives The Joy a shove. From deep in the Land of Nod, The Joy says, "What?"

"Sleeping Beauty. It's almost time. You're gonna miss it."

The Joy shakes it off, sits up and looks at the TV. On screen, the grid of runners is now displaying graphics of medals over the finishers.

JACKSON'S APARTMENT

Jackson has his lounger sitting upright. He leans forward as he watches his friend approach the finish. He thinks about how proud he is of all of them. This is a great thing.

SHAD & BENJI'S APARTMENT

With enthusiasm, Benji says, "For the last time, I say...Twenty. Turn around."

With that, Shad makes the turn for home. He's so excited to be heading for the virtual finish line that he can't contain himself. Breathlessly he says, "This is for everyone who doesn't just hope for better. This is for all of us who rise up to do something about it."

STEPH'S APARTMENT

To camera, Steph says, "And we're about to watch Shad Perkins, co-founder of the *We Are One Marathon In Place* cross the finish. Just a few more steps."

Steph puts her hand to her ear as a voice comes to her through her headset. The look of excitement drops from her face. To the voice in her ear she says, "What was that?"

JACKSON'S APARTMENT

Sitting on the edge of his lounge chair, Jackson watches as his dear friend is about to be bathed in personal victory.

On TV, the screen cuts away from Shad to a red, white and blue graphic for breaking news. Serious music follows. A voice over says: "This is a breaking news story."

The network anchor looks gravely into camera. "This is Bruce Manchester, reporting from Minneapolis. All four officers involved in the George Floyd killing have just been fired. I repeat, all four of the officers involved in the George Floyd killing have just been fired. Murder charges may follow."

IF YOU ENJOYED THIS BOOK...

Thanks for enjoying *Careful-ish*. It's always a thrill to know a reader enjoys a book as much as I enjoyed writing it.

Being a self-published author means lifting all your own boxes. A little support is always appreciated. Telling your friends and people on Amazon is one of the most powerful things you can do to keep this machine moving.

If you want to write a review on Amazon, I'll be eternally grateful.

To be kept in the loop on *Careful-ish* events, sequels, and other things Honey Parker, visit **www.HoneyParkerBooks.com** and join the mailing list.

If you'd like to join the Careful-ish group on Facebook, it's free and fun and public and full of all kinds of un-masked frolic. You'll find it at **https://www.facebook.com/groups/carefulish**.

Thanks so much for caring-ish.

ACKNOWLEDGMENTS

Tremendous thanks to Beth Hoppe, for making sure the news side of things stayed within the realm of possibly possible—as well as for *Call The Midwife* and *The Great British Baking Show*, two civilized *programmes* that saved me from other things. Bill Howe, for playing the part of The Curmudgeon. Downtown Jonnie D., you provided more facts about finance than my small brain could absorb, and you have a catch-phrase you let me steal. Jennifer Squillante, your tales of boots on the ground were invaluable. Thanks to Dave Franco for being a both patient and enthusiastic editor. Kim Klopp, you demonstrated the best way ever to climb onto a bar stool. Renie Glassman, this challah's for you. Jackie and Jeff Brown, you are great sounding boards and always provide the perfect wine pairing. Jerry Cohn, thanks for coloring so much of who I am. Janet Murphy, thank you for exactly what you'd think. Blaine Parker, for my world.

ABOUT THE AUTHOR

Careful-ish is Honey Parker's first novel, but not her first words. She's often surprised to find she has co-authored several business books. She's also written and sold several screenplays which, as per Hollywood tradition, are circling various levels of that place known as Development Hell. A veteran advertising writer and creative director for big agencies in New York and Los Angeles, she eventually co-founded her own creative shop in Park City, Utah. Somewhere in the middle of all that, Honey began doing standup comedy in clubs and on TV, and once claimed the title Funniest Person In Advertising. Her greatest disappointment is that the title came with neither a sash nor cash.

Honey is married to her best friend and business partner, Blaine Parker. Or, as Honey's father refers to him, "The man who took her off the market." In their spare time, Honey & Blaine have run an ad agency, spoken to small-business owners around the globe about profitable branding, and co-hosted the weekly podcast, CoupleCo: Working With Your Spouse For Fun & Profit. As the most amateur of athletes, they've raced together in full and half marathons and triathlons. Honey's other "accomplishments" include being a performer at various Club Med locations around the world, sailing in the North American Fireball Championships despite the fact she cannot sail, and sparring with the world female boxing champ, a feat for which Honey is most proud that she neither bled nor cried.

You can find Honey online at www.HoneyParkerBooks.com

Made in the USA
Columbia, SC
26 August 2022